The Wisdom of
Religious Commitment

The Wisdom of
Religious Commitment

Terrence W. Tilley

GEORGETOWN UNIVERSITY PRESS / WASHINGTON, D.C.

Georgetown University Press, Washington, D.C.
© 1995 by Georgetown University Press. All rights reserved.
Printed in the United States of America
10 9 8 7 6 5 4 3 2 1   1995
THE VOLUME IS PRINTED ON ACID-FREE OFFSET BOOK PAPER

Library of Congress Cataloging-in-Publication Data

Tilley, Terrence W.
    The wisdom of religious commitment / Terrence W. Tilley.
        p.   cm.
    Includes bibliographical references and index.
    1. Religion—Philosophy. 2. Wisdom—Religious aspects.
    I. Title.
    BL51.T56   1995
    210—dc20
    ISBN 0-87840-580-1   181756   94-32280

For Elena and Christine
of whom I am very proud
and to whom I am very grateful
for teaching me so much about practical wisdom

Contents

Acknowledgments

This book has developed slowly and many of its parts were explored in a variety of venues. Earlier versions of some parts were also published as essays in various places. I thank the various editors and publishers for permission to rework material for use here. I also thank those who commented on the papers; I learned much from them (perhaps not enough), and my acknowledgment of their generous assistance cannot be presumed to claim that they endorse the position argued herein or any of its parts.

A very early and rough version of material now in chapters 3, 4, and 5 was presented as "Permissive Parity Arguments and the Prudence of Religious Commitment" to a Workshop on Skepticism and Fideism, Center for Philosophy of Religion, hosted by the University of Notre Dame with support from the Society of Christian Philosophers in May 1986. Philip Quinn, the director of the workshop, and George Mavrodes (among others) offered substantial challenges which caused me to revise my views significantly. An intermediate truncated version was published as "The Prudence of Religious Commitment," *Horizons* 16 (Spring, 1989). A further revised version of this material, along with some of the material now in chapters 1 and 2 was discussed in the Philosophy of Religion Section at the Annual Convention of the College Theology Society at Saint Mary's College, Moraga, California, in June 1993 as "The Body in Religious Epistemology: 'Masses and Holy Water,' and the Ethics of Belief." Michael Barnes, John McCarthy, Gerald McCarthy, and Steve Ostovich offered substantial criticism and forced me again to rethink and revise material now in chapters 4 and 5. Portions of material now in chapter 1 were read under various titles to a Florida State University Philosophy Department Colloquium in October 1993, and to the Annual Meeting of the Society for Philosophy of Religion in Savannah, Georgia, in February 1994. There, my respondent, Richard Creel (along with William Alston and Dewi Z. Phillips, among others), offered valuable suggestions. Much of chapter 1 was discussed in the theological methodology section at the Annual Meeting of the Catholic Theological Society of America in Baltimore in June 1994. A rather different version of material from chapter 1 was published as "In Favor of a 'Practical Theory' of Religion: Montaigne and Pascal," in *Theology without Foundations*, ed. Stanley Hauerwas, Nancey Murphy, and Mark Nation (Nashville: Abingdon, 1994). An earlier version of part of chapter 3 was published as "Religious Pluralism as a Problem for 'Practical' Religious Epistemology," in *Religious Studies* 30(2) (June, 1994).

I also am most appreciative of the academic institutions that have supported my work: Saint Michael's College in Vermont and the Florida State University. My students and colleagues at both institutions have been encouraging and helpfully critical and I am grateful to them. My gratitude remains even as I take up the duties of professor and chairperson of religious studies at the University of Dayton in the fall of 1994.

At the Georgetown University Press, director John Samples and production manager Patricia Rayner have led a team that has made this a clearer and more coherent work. Whatever elegance the book has owes much to them. Mary Sartor, SND, graduate assistant at the University of Dayton helped prepare the index. Joanne Beirise, Marietta Geray, OSB, and the office team at the University of Dayton also helped in uncountable ways to make it possible for me to attend to work on this book.

The "suffering spouse" who stands behind this book is the patient and supportive Maureen A. Tilley. Our partnership is *conditio sine qua non* for all my work. The dedication is to our daughters who have endured having two parents in academia. They have taught me far more, I suspect, than they imagine they have.

The Wisdom of
Religious Commitment

Introduction

Skepticism has dominated much modern philosophy of religion. Skepticism about religious belief surfaces in courses in philosophy of religion taught in the secular academy, especially in the United States. All too often these courses have been taught in two steps. First, the philosopher knocks down the proofs of the existence of God. Since the proofs fail, the rational move for the smart student is to suspend judgment about the belief that God exists. Second, the philosopher shows that no theist has provided a credible theodicy, a theory to explain how so many evils permeate a world allegedly created by an all-powerful, all-knowing, all-good God. The rational move for the student is not to believe in a God since that belief is undermined by the reality of evils. Thus, the modern student should be skeptical. None ought to believe in God—or engage in religious practices.

In effect, religious skeptics from David Hume in the eighteenth century through Bertrand Russell, Antony Flew, J. L. Mackie, and Kai Nielsen in the twentieth have set the terms of the discourse in philosophy of religion, at least in the English-speaking academic context. Numerous philosophers who were themselves actively religious, for example, Thomas Reid, John Henry Newman, Friedrich von Hügel, and some of the British Idealists, challenged the dominant trend and refused to accept the terms of the discourse. Their works were often ignored in the dominant tradition. It is not surprising. Modernity has been characterized by a flight from authorities, especially religious authorities, and a quest for autonomy, especially intellectual autonomy. Modern philosophers of religion reflect and encourage that turn.

Religiously committed philosophers working in the dominant tradition have generally been on the defensive. They have spilt much ink defending belief in God from skeptical attacks. Some have engaged in "rational theology," the attempt to prove religious propositions using rational arguments alone. Others take up "rational apologetics," the attempt to show that religious believers are more warranted in holding their religious beliefs than are their atheistic or agnostic opponents. Rational apologetics is often based on individuals' having religious experiences which supposedly provide a foundation for religious belief. But, alas, the apologists tend to achieve only rational defenses, showing that religious believers are within their rights to *hold on to* the beliefs they have. All too often, the religiously committed philosopher makes little headway in showing that anyone interested in the love of wisdom ought to *take up* religious belief or practice. Perhaps it is because the discourse practice of modern philosophy makes religious and anti-religious partisans seem like disembodied minds debating a purely academic subject or like quarreling lawyers scoring points in a debating society.

Yet there is another, and, I think, a better way.

Another strand in the philosophy of religion emerged in the Enlightenment. Instead of walking with skeptics to explain how religious beliefs are justified, it seeks to understand the wisdom of religious commitment. Mainstream philosophers have typically dismissed this tradition as irrationalist or fideist (see Penelhum 1983). However, it is better understood as a "practical" philosophy of religion, rooted in the insights of Michel de Montaigne and Blaise Pascal. Exploring the shape of this tradition and displaying its strengths over the dominant skeptical discourse in modern philosophy of religion occupies chapter 1.

Mainstream philosophy of religion tends to ignore religion as practiced. It deals only with the intellectual element of religion, religious beliefs. A religion, however, is more than individuals' believing that God exists, and religious practice is more than belief. Seeking to understand the wisdom of religious commitment requires asking about religious practices. While the mainstream has debated propositions such as "There is a God" completely abstracted from the religious practices in which they are at home, a practical philosophy of religion requires attending to religion as a whole. Chapter 2 invokes the contemporary academic study of religion to examine what constitutes a religion—a necessary step for a practical understanding of religion that goes beyond theoretical explanation of religious beliefs.

Yet the mainstream pattern cannot and ought not be dismissed. In recent years it has become more aware of the philosophical importance of religious practice. The third chapter examines the work of three exemplary contemporary philosophers of religion. Richard Swinburne argues for the rational superiority of theism over materialism. Alvin Plantinga argues that theists' beliefs are more warranted than atheistic materialists' beliefs. William Alston argues that Christians develop beliefs through Christian practices and that participating in those practices is reasonable because Christian practices cannot be shown to be significantly less reliable than perception. As I am a typical participant in modern academic debates, I will unreservedly critique the weaknesses I see in these approaches. But as I am also a practical philosopher, I will unhesitatingly collect whatever insights I can to bolster my attempt to go beyond them in chapters 4 and 5 in order to understand the wisdom of religious commitment.

Chapter 4 begins by showing the true strengths and inevitable limits of the modern approaches. It then displays narratively the practice of wisdom. Wisdom is a virtue: Aristotle called it *phronesis*; St. Thomas Aquinas designated it *prudentia*; John Henry Newman wrote of an "illative sense." For Aristotle *phronesis* is a "bridge virtue," a virtue that links the moral and intellectual virtues. In brief, *phronesis* is the ability to put intellect into action. Properly, people of practical wisdom avoid the pitfalls of rashness in action and of refraining when they should act. Virtues, however, are properly not argued about, but shown. Consequently, chapter 4 will display increasingly accomplished exercises of the virtue of practical wisdom. In and through the display of this virtue, one can discern some guidelines for its proper practice.

Chapter 5 then moves to the wisdom of religious commitment. How can a wise person hold or take up a religion in all its complexity (as displayed in chapter 2)? This chapter seeks a path far more "embodied" than the usual academic debates of modern philosophy; it seeks to discern a pattern in (or to abstract a pattern from) the practice of wisely making or keeping a commitment to religious practices within religious communities shaped and carried by religious institutions. Because wisdom is a virtue that must be concretely displayed, chapter 5 spends substantial space on specific religious and theological practices as paradigms of the issues involved in developing an understanding of the wisdom of making a religious commitment.

A short epilogue brings the book to a practical conclusion. It shows how the tradition of Montaigne and Pascal, properly developed, is a path one can walk to understand the wisdom of religious commitment. That path is not simple, or easy, but it is liberating and practical. It takes us nearer to our goal of understanding than the mainstream pattern.

Along with my previous book, *The Evils of Theodicy* (1991), this book addresses a central area of debate in modern philosophy of religion. It argues that the shape of the modern discourse is important, but finally distorted and misleading. The solution to the problems of evil, I argued in the *Evils of Theodicy*, was not to be found by con-- structing better arguments, but by engaging in better practices. The "hidden agenda" of the present book, revealed especially in its last chapter and epilogue, is to show that properly engaging in liberating and empowering practices constitutes, in part, the making of a wise religious commitment. In sum, I have found that real solutions to "the problem of evil" and the real solutions to the problem of the "rationality of religious belief," the two foci of modern philosophy of religion and of many courses in philosophy of religion, are the same.

1

Toward a Practical Philosophy of Religion

THE CONSTRUAL OF RELIGION AND RELIGIOUS BELIEF IN MODERN PHILOSOPHY

Since the beginning of modernity, philosophers of religion have focused their attention on religious beliefs abstracted from religious life. Their debates over "religion" typically have failed to address the practical issues an embodied person faces, but have attended almost exclusively to issues of pure rational theology suitable for the academic mind alone. Philosophers have endlessly debated the proofs of the existence of God, the problems of theodicy, the rationality of holding religious beliefs, and the possibility of determining whether religious beliefs are meaningful. Most current philosophical explorations of the reliability or justifiability of religious beliefs have continued this tradition of ignoring the practical questions about people participating in the life of a religion. Because modern philosophers abstract religious beliefs from religious life and focus on the former without regard to the latter, their attempts to construct philosophies of religion are deformed: They say practically nothing about religion as it is practiced.

Philosophers of religion are not alone in ignoring the significance of religious life while debating about religious beliefs. William A. Clebsch (1979) captured the problem clearly and elegantly; he contrasted conservative apologetics for religious belief in the modern era with the rich religious life of the premodern epochs:

> Religious belief stridently affirming the inerrancy of a miscellaneous assortment of interwoven and overlaid writings was hardly the same as religious life proceeding unself-consciously under the power of certain myths told in those writings. Religious belief denying human cousinhood with simians can hardly be compared with religious life straightforwardly delighting in brotherhood with a god-man. Religious belief trying to hold

5

Christ in the status of a redeemer differed from religious life humbly serving an incarnate and resurrected savior (246).

Clebsch here reminds us that religious life cannot be reduced to religious beliefs. Nor is it clear that arguing over the propositional content of those beliefs can stand in for understanding, analyzing, and criticizing religions and religious life. Whether conservative or progressive, most investigations of "reason and religion" have remained mired in abstract debates about "religious beliefs," or intellectual wrangling over the existence of God. They have ignored the far more important question of the reasonableness or wisdom of participation in the richness and complexity of religious life.[1]

Religious epistemology is the center of modern philosophy of religion. Investigations in this area have generally remained bound to the modern focus on religious beliefs as properties or dispositions of individuals without regard to their socially embodied religious life.[2] The individualism and anti-authoritarianism of modernity appear especially in arguments over the foundations of religious belief. If a person's belief is well-founded in the nature of things, based on good evidence or irresistible experience, concluded from a good argument, formed in a reliable belief-forming practice, or developed by the exercise of a properly functioning belief-forming "mechanism" working in a suitable environment, then that individual (or that individual's belief) is justified, warranted, proper. If the nature of things does not properly evoke a religious belief, or if the evidence for one's religious hypothesis is inconclusive, or if one's religious experience is unreliable, or if one's argument for the existence of God is not sound or probable, or if one's religious doxastic practice is not reliable or not properly followed, or if one's belief-forming equipment is not performing as it should or is not in the proper environment when one develops a religious belief, then that individual or that belief would not be warranted, justified, proper, etc. The question of an individual's entitlement to hold specific propositions about religious matters remains the central area of concern in religious epistemology (see Tilley 1992).

Religious epistemologists have tended to accept the modern era's valorization of the individual's quest for cognitive certainty. Yet the modern quest for certainty was not a philosophical Athena sprung full-grown from Descartes' head in the middle of the seventeenth century. Modern philosophy, including philosophy of religion, grew out of a tradition in which theology was "scientia," sure knowledge. From the "golden age" of the thirteenth-century scholastics through Calvin's *Institutes* in the sixteenth century and into the modern period, the theologians' ideal was the formation of a comprehensive *summa* or system of Christian theological beliefs. But by the end of the sixteenth century, there were many systems in irreconcilable conflict; and by the middle of the early seventeenth century, the tolerance portrayed in Montaigne's *Essays* and inscribed in the Edict of Nantes (1598) had become untenable. Each of the many other forms of Christian faith became as much a "disconfirming other" for one's own faith as the Jewish tradition had been. Thus, the intellectual elite's "flight from authority" and the quest for *individual* certainty which constitutes the Enlightenment project was a flight from *competing* authorities, *conflicting* systems, irreconcilable *scientiae*, and religious institutions *at war* with each other. The prima facie problem that modern philosophers of religion have addressed is the rationality of religious beliefs. But given the social context of early modernity, a period of profound social conflict, economic upheaval, and religious strife, the real problems were practical ones. The intellectuals' quest for certainty is just one facet of a cultural longing for security, in this case a security found by each becoming his own authority.[3]

Another pithy paragraph from William A. Clebsch illustrates the practical problems a person might face in that era:

> Imagine yourself a law-abiding Londoner born in 1615 and destined to live seventy-five years. You are baptized an Anglican and raised to tolerate mild Puritans in your church. As a teenager you turn very high-church, and when you are married you are ready to force Anglo-Catholicism on the unwilling Scots. You raise your young children Presbyterians, but as they grow up you turn Congregationalist. In middle age you revert to moderate Anglicanism, then ripen into a crypto-Roman Catholic like your king. Before you die you are a generous, if somewhat bored, Anglican again, having been told it would not much matter if you had turned Baptist. In your lifetime you have paid taxes to support Protestant kings against parliament and parliament against the same kings, to finance civil war and regicide, then to restore the lineage of the king who was executed, and finally to arrange a *coup d'état* against that lineage.
>
> The instance is extreme, for you were living in an age of extremes (Clebsch 1979:187).

Pastors would advise you, according to Clebsch, to turn away from religious traditions, communities, and institutions in order to cultivate "the real stuff" of religion: pious feelings or moral behavior.

Intellectuals, however, 'solved' such problems by turning to abstraction. They debated beliefs which had little to do with common life. For instance, in 1697, William King, Anglican Archbishop of Dublin, wrote a treatise on the philosophical problem of evil ("How does evil originate in a world created and governed by an all-powerful, all-knowing, all-good Deity?"). The treatise, however, ignores the religious wars that racked Ireland and England, the evils wars generate, the division of Ireland into plantations which redistributed land from Irish peasant to English landlord, and even King's own stint as a prisoner of war less than a decade earlier (see Tilley 1991:225–26). King, finally positioned comfortably with a gentleman's living in Dublin, could concentrate on evil as an abstract intellectual problem, not a burning threat to his life and freedom.

Modern philosophers of religion have inherited the systematic theologians' approach to resolving religious conflicts. Theologians were—and mostly are—concerned with showing which are the right (doctrinal) beliefs. Practical questions are ignored or shunted to irrelevance. Philosophical rhetoric sometimes has so divided epistemic from "prudential" or "moral" issues that they seemed to have nothing to do with each other (see Alston 1982). Religious epistemology developed in debate over whether individuals properly can and do have certainty when they hold religious beliefs. Its practitioners have usually tacitly accepted the basic presumptions of modernity: (1) having abandoned authority, each individual properly quests for her or his own certainty; and (2) religious belief is a "private" affair involving individuals and their beliefs. That the quest for certainty and the turn to the private individual were responses to a general cultural upheaval is often thought to be irrelevant.

The academic study of religion and some recent developments in epistemology have shown that the issues are far more complex than the modern paradigm can comfortably accommodate. In our era, religious affiliation may be, at least politically, a matter of individual choice and not subject to the frequent shifts in allegiance of Clebsch's imaginary "law-abiding Londoner." However, such political freedom does not imply that individuals can choose their beliefs freely. Nor is showing that individuals are entitled to hold specific propositions necessary or sufficient to show the reasonableness of their religious commitments, practices, and beliefs. Philosophy of religion in general and religious epistemology need a new practical paradigm for thinking about religion in the concrete.

The way forward begins by stepping back to retrieve the practical insights of a tradition sadly vilified in much modern philosophy of religion, the tradition of Montaigne and Pascal. We need not reject the gains of modernity (as some postliberal theologians and postmodern philosophers do). We do not need to intensify modern individualism and atomization (as some poststructuralist philosophers and literary theorists do; see Tilley, 1995). Rather, we need to recognize both the contributions and the incompleteness of the modern project in philosophy of religion. A practical philosophy of religion recognizes the social, institutional, and practical dimensions of life without neglecting religious belief. But a practical philosophy of religion focuses on religious believing as practices of *embodied* persons, not on propositions to be debated by minds engaged in academic exercises. In short, we need to make central the notion that people *practice* their religion.

A practical philosophy of religion finds that understanding the reasonableness of religious belief and practice does not fall into the realm of *scientia* and certainty, but into that of *praxis* and *phronesis*.[4] Religion is not merely a set of beliefs or even a theological or doctrinal system. Religious knowing or believing is not merely accepting doctrines, but living a life shaped by religious practices. Part of participating in the practices of a religious tradition, of course, is learning the beliefs which that practice carries or transmits. But coming to hold doctrinal beliefs is part of, not a foundation for, the practice. Being justified in one's believing is not having warranted basic or foundational beliefs, but having the ability to make and to keep a wise commitment to a religious life and to live it fully. The real challenge is not to resolve abstract puzzles about theological propositions, but to solve the problem of the wise choice of practices, including those practices that generate beliefs. That is the purpose of a *practical* philosophy of religion.

Feminist 'epistemologists'[5] point the way in this area for epistemology generally. First, some note that a great gulf separates academic epistemologies from real issues. "Feminists who expect a theory of knowledge to address people's everyday cognitive experiences and to examine the place of knowledge in people's lives, who expect it to produce analyses and strategies that will contribute to the construction of a world fit for human habitation, can find little enlightenment in mainstream epistemology" (Code 1991:267). Academic epistemologies especially neglect the difficulties that people have in getting access to positions in which basic information is available. They are blind to, or think irrelevant, class, race, and gender issues. Academic epistemologies ignore the political and social realities that make the very possibility of knowing a practical impossibility for those marginalized in a society and unable to get into position to be able to know.

Being in position to know something is, in general, taken for granted by epistemologists. They simply presume that what I will label "positional defects" are limited to individuals' epistemic defects, disqualifications or deviations from the "normal case." For instance, a blind person cannot get into a position of "being appeared to redly" and a deaf person cannot get into position "now hearing a high-pitched tone." These are taken to be "equipment defects" that obviously disqualify people with "defective equipment" from being in position to perceive sights or sounds. Such so-called defects render them irrelevant to academic epistemology. They are simply not subjects in and of that discourse. A person who was neither at the royal banquet last night nor has received any reports of what happened at the banquet is in no position to know how many glasses of red wine the queen drank. This is not an equipment defect, but an access problem. Since the person had no access to the relevant information, the question of her knowing or not knowing the proposition about the queen's drinking simply never comes up—it remains irrelevant to and out of sight in epistemology. In general, such "positional defects" are perhaps benignly, although all too blithely, covered by *ceteris paribus* or other similar qualifications or taken to be of the same order as "equipment defects."

Yet "other things being equal" does not always apply benignly and ought not be invoked blithely. Social and political practices can also give people positional defects, a factor ignored in academic epistemology. Marginalized people are also not subjects of and in that discourse. Code persuasively cites the problems that women on welfare in Canada (and, analogously, in other nations) have in getting access to services and information as an example of systemic epistemological marginalization. It is not that these women are stupid or lazy or unindustrious, but that the varied demands made on them to acquire and maintain the assistance that they need to provide their families with basic needs also makes it impossible for them to get in position to acquire the information they need to find a way off the eternal wheel of welfare. When one is required by welfare rules, for instance, to spend the entire day riding buses to follow the regulations for getting to locations where one can obtain needed medical assistance, that same day cannot be used to find a job or child care or to acquire information or education.

The fact is that political, social, ethnic, economic, and gender-based patterns, however benignly intended, make it practically impossible for people to get into position to know. Such disqualifications can be malignant in effect. Nor are they the same sort of "positional defects" noted previously. That I could not find out the time of an interview for a job for which I am qualified because I was required by law or regulation to be elsewhere is a "positional defect," but not one due to my own intrinsic epistemic defect or my (uninteresting) lack of information, but to my being systematically forced to an epistemically marginal position. *Ceteris paribus* clauses obscure such practical epistemic problems.

Of course, the epistemologist will claim that such problems are irrelevant to the proper task of epistemology, of finding the conditions under which a person can be said to know. And that may be true. But the fact that it is true is the very problem. The problem is that the "proper task" of epistemology is blind to the (contingent, but real and extensive) social factors that empower or disable an embodied, socially located person from getting in position to know. The only subject of the discourse of academic epistemology is the epistemically privileged individual who has no specific social location and no difficulty with access to basic data or information. The real subject of academic epistemology is the disembodied mind. But such a subject cannot exist. Only within the ivory towers of academia does academic epistemology apply. At best, epistemologists study rare cases, not common ones. Religious epistemologists have followed their academic colleagues by making the subject of their discourse equally disembodied. Their work has the same problems.

Second, in addition to introducing practical, political elements into epistemology, some feminists advocate the demythologization of the Enlightenment myth that there can be dispassionate investigations, even in science. Alison M. Jaggar (1989) has noted that "western epistemology has tended to view emotion with suspicion and even hostility" (154). She goes on to note the consequences of obliterating emotions:

This derogatory western attitude toward emotion, like the earlier western contempt for sensory observation [now so basic to epistemology], fails to recognize that emotion, like sensory perception, is necessary to human survival. Emotions prompt us to act appropriately, to approach some people and situations and to avoid others, to caress or cuddle, fight or flee. Without emotion, human life would be unthinkable. Moreover, emotions have an intrinsic as well as an instrumental value. Although not all emotions are enjoyable or even justifiable . . . life without any emotion would be life without any meaning (154–55).

Jaggar claims that even positivist epistemologies allow a role for emotion in the (intuitive) suggestion of hypotheses for investigation, but rigorously exclude emotion from the processes of justification. However, if (as in the naturalized epistemologies typical of Quine [1985], Goldman [1986], Plantinga, and others) one cannot separate the processes of belief formation from the processes of belief justification, then an epistemology of science itself must incorporate "values and emotions. Moreover, such an incorporation seems a necessary feature of all knowledge and conceptions of knowledge"(Jaggar 1989:156). The upshot is that affect, inclination, intuition, or emotion must be internalized into epistemology, especially into the naturalized epistemologies that focus on cognitional or doxastic (belief-forming) practices.

The simple fact is that pure academic epistemologies have been found wanting as accounts of human knowing both because they fail to explain belief acquisition and because they fail to show the conditions for actual knowing. The modern separation of epistemic from moral and prudential issues is not merely misguided. It is, rather, a symptom of the philosophical disease of modernity where pure theory is valorized and practical, bodily, emotional issues degraded, where the socially privileged subject is taken as the norm, and where the social locations that shape us are blithely and not benignly erased. Nevertheless, some contemporary epistemologists have embarked on a practical path that must lead them to consider doxastic practices, the conditions under which they work, and the "noncognitive" ingredients of knowing, including both personal attitudes and social conditions.

Religious epistemologists like William Alston have begun to make this turn and have started opening this path. Ultimately it leads to a claim that the justification of religious belief is best understood not as demonstrating that an individual is entitled to hold some specific religious proposition, but as showing the wisdom of participating in a religious tradition, and, by implication, the wisdom of accepting the central and distinctive practices and convictions of that tradition.

The dominant strand in modern philosophy of religion has presumed what I will describe in chapter 3 as the "presumption of substitutability." It substitutes examining the validity of an isolated, unlocated individual's cognition or mental holding of "religious beliefs" for understanding religion. In chapter 4 we will find a better way, a path that renews a somewhat neglected tradition in the modern philosophy of religion, the practices of Montaigne and Pascal.

THE LEGACY OF MONTAIGNE

Michel de Montaigne, in his "Apology for Raymond Sebond" (1580), wrote that "Christians do themselves harm in trying to support their belief by human reasons, since it is conceived only by faith and by a particular inspiration of divine grace"(121). Montaigne here seems to anticipate the two basic patterns that would come to dominate the modern debates over the justification of religion and religious belief for the next four centuries.

The first pattern can be labeled *externalist*: If reason could provide a solid external foundation or uncover external evidences for religion or show the validity of a revelation, then a reasonable person could and should accept religious beliefs thus externally warranted. Conversely, if rational arguments cannot provide independent or external reasons for accepting religious claims or can show religious beliefs to be irrational, then a reasonable person is not justified in accepting religious beliefs. The dominant tradition in modern philosophy of religion is externalist.

The second pattern can be called *internalist*: Rational arguments cannot be expected to provide an external basis for religion so religious belief properly must rest on faith and grace alone. Whatever reasonableness or evidence can be found in religion is found within, not before or under, religious commitment.[6] The dominant tradition generally characterizes this view as "fideist" or "irrationalist."

Montaigne himself has generally been classed with the internalists. He is typically identified as a fideist who is skeptical of reason's power to ascertain religious truth and who advocates conformity to prevailing wind of tradition as the appropriate stance to take in the absence of good external reasons to be religious (see Penelhum 1983). He can thus be envisioned as standing near the head of a line which runs through Pascal, Demea (in Hume's *Dialogues Concerning Natural Religion*), and Kierkegaard, and extends to D. Z. Phillips and others in our own time. These internalists do not isolate faith from reason or religion from the rest of the world, as their opponents sometimes claim. Nonetheless, they do find that religious beliefs need no evidence and have no external rational support. Religion is a matter of grace, faith, committed choice, or expressive reaction to the world. Reasoning and evidence are internal to faith, not its foundations. No external warrants or arguments can or should apply.

The "subject" of Montaigne's essay, the late fifteenth-century author Raymond Sebond, can be seen as an ancestor of the externalists. This dominant modern tradition includes the numerous rational theologians of the seventeenth century, Cleanthes and Philo (in Hume's *Dialogues*), William Paley, and extends more recently through A. J. Ayer, Bertrand Russell, Frederick Copleston, Antony Flew, Hugo Meynell, Richard Swinburne, and others. In different ways, such thinkers presume that religious belief needs evidential support or foundational demonstration if a reasonable person is to accept it. They then disagree about whether it has any such support or whether the foundations of theism are sturdy enough to support the religious edifice. To be religious, and more specifically to be Christian, may ultimately be a matter of divine grace; but human reason must at least prepare the way of the Lord.

Yet Montaigne hinted at a possible third approach in an earlier essay, "We should meddle soberly with judging divine ordinances" (1574), an approach, alas, mostly unexplored in philosophy of religion. In this essay Montaigne recollects a dispute over the rationality of believing in divine providence. But here the ground is not the fertile soil where either externalist disputes over whether one should accept God's existence or internalist rhetoric about simple acceptance, divine grace, or leaps of faith flourish. The context for this essay is not a dispute between belief and unbelief, but a dispute over established patterns of religious practice. The dispute is particular, not general, and practical, not theoretical. Here a rather different pattern and practice of argument emerges.

The argument is about evidence for a belief that God acts in history (an argument that seems externalist), but it presumes the reality of and belief in God (a pattern that makes the argument seem internalist). Montaigne's discussion of "sober meddling" reaches the following judgment about the disputes between contending Protestants and Catholics:

> It is enough for a Christian to believe that all things come from God, to receive them with acknowledgment of his divine

and inscrutable wisdom, and therefore to take them in good part, in whatever aspect they may be sent to him. But I think that the practice I see is bad, of trying to strengthen and support our religion by the good fortune and prosperity of our enterprises. Our belief has enough other foundations; it does not need events to authorize it. For when the people are accustomed to these arguments, which are plausible and suited to their taste, there is a danger that when in turn contrary and disadvantageous events come, this will shake their faith. Thus, in the wars we are engaged in for the sake of religion, those [Protestants] who had the advantage in the encounter [i.e., the battle] at La Rochelabeille make much ado about this incident and use their good fortune as sure approbation of their party; but when they come later to excuse their misfortunes at Moncontour and Jarnac as being fatherly scourges and chastisements, unless they have their following completely at their mercy, they make the people sense readily enough that this is getting two grinding fees for one sack, and blowing hot and cold with the same mouth. It would be better to tell them the true foundations of the truth (160).

The situation Montaigne describes is not one in which believers seek a theoretical foundation or evidence for their faith. Rather, each of two warring groups of believers, Huguenot and Catholic, attempts to develop evidence to show that God is on their side. Each can begin by pointing to a military victory as a sign of divine favor for their cause. Yet when each loses a battle it is not a sign of divine displeasure with their cause or favor for the opponents' cause, but a God-given chastisement of the side the divine providence favors. Montaigne rightly mocks the self-serving dissymmetry of theological apologies which can construe all events as evidence in support of one's own cause.

It would be easy to construe this account as internalist. Montaigne's skepticism of the Protestants' arguments (and, implicitly of Catholics' analogous arguments) would be another instance of his own skepticism about external support for religion. Like religious externalists' arguments, such evidential claims and counterclaims are inconclusive at best, obscurantist and deceptive at worst. Montaigne seems to take a skeptical approach akin to that in mainstream modern philosophy of religion.

Yet when one considers the actual dispute Montaigne recollects, it is not typical of the disputes that fire internalists' rhetoric or externalists' theoretical arguments. The issues are not "religion" or "religious belief" in general, or the existence or nonexistence of God. Their dispute is over *which* Christian tradition is divinely sanctioned. The context is not an academic philosophical dispute, but a bitter conflict within a family of traditions that share some practices and goals, and a war among the institutions that support them. The audience for the arguments, as Montaigne notes, is not academic skeptics, but already committed believers. Each side tries to find arguments that believers on the other side or wavering believers on their own might find plausible as supports for their allegiance. The proponents typically appeal to shared beliefs and images, especially biblical ones, which carry substantial rhetorical weight for adherents in both camps. The envisioned audience for such persuasion is not the ignorant masses which elegant rhetoric can easily sway, but people of common sense. Montaigne advises against such "evidential" arguments because the audience might well be able to "see through" their ideological dissymmetry and find their faith shaken when events conspire against their party.

This species of argument is not usually found in mainstream philosophy of religion, but in inter-Christian polemics. It is a pattern of argument that often degenerates into name-calling, proof-texting, and finger-pointing almost before it begins. Sadly lacking here are the issues of rationality, evidence and argument that light the internalist-externalist fires.

However degenerate the arguments themselves become, the questions they address are important and practical. Within which form of life ought the hearers live? Which practices ought the audience take up? To which tradition and institution ought they give their allegiance? Internalists' urging them to fideism begs the question when the issue is *which* faith one ought practice. After all, appealing to faith when the dispute is about *faiths* is like appealing to authority when the dispute is about authorities. The externalists' quest to find evidence is also useless for the evidence is ambiguous at best. Neither approach can help with this practical problem. Those who propose these arguments may claim that they aren't trying to solve practical problems. And that is precisely the problem—they are impractical. Their strategies are irrelevant to help resolve the practical disputes.

Moreover, a practical approach doesn't misportray the situation of commitment as internalist or externalist approaches do. The internalists tend to take religious commitment as basic, unarguable, *given*. Like classic Protestant doctrines of predestination and divine grace in which the person has no say over her true status vis-à-vis God, so internalism finds that no ordinary human practices make it possible to give the person a say in *taking* a position or *making* a commitment. But the fact is that people do choose to make commitments in religion as in love; even if we cannot freely choose our beliefs or our lusts does not imply that we do not, cannot, or should not commit ourselves to active religious devotion or to chaste marriage. Having beliefs or lusts may be necessary, but is surely not sufficient, for justifying engaging in religious or amatory practices.

The externalists tend to portray the position of the disputants as similar to scientific neutrality in which neutral investigators seek evidence and in which the convictions the investigators hold are irrelevant. This view is most fully developed by Flew (1976) as his methodological presumption of atheism. The argument ought to proceed, Flew claims, on analogy with the presumption of innocence in a criminal trial. The burden of proof is on the one who wants to prove something, that is, on the prosecution or the theist. We presume "innnocence" until the defendant is proven guilty, "atheism" until God is proven real. If the burden of proof isn't met, then we revert to the presumption in each case. But that position is simply untenable. The fact is that the investigators are not neutral judges but committed disputants. The issue is not one of simply adding a new belief (belief in God) to our store of already-accepted beliefs, but the question of which beliefs are the central and distinctive convictions that we ought to hold (compare Tilley 1978:12–18 on Flew). Both internalist and externalist accounts misportray the practical-intellectual issues.

But if the usual philosophical approaches are not only wrong in their presumptions about the positions of those practically engaged in argument, but also of little use in practical disputes, is there no practice for resolving overarching and life-determining practical issues except the desultory polemics and the self-serving rhetoric whose posturing is open to Montaigne's withering analysis? Montaigne himself hinted at a different way of disputing such important practical issues. This path avoids not only the antitheses of externalism and internalism, but also the dead end of polemics. In an essay "On the art of discussion" (1588), he offered a practical prescription for a practical disease:

> The most fruitful and natural exercise of our mind, in my opinion, is discussion. I find it sweeter than any other action of our life. . . .

> The study of books is a languishing and feeble activity that gives no heat, whereas discussion teaches and exercises us at the same time. If I discuss with a strong mind and a stiff jouster, he presses on my flanks, prods me right and left; his ideas launch mine. Rivalry, glory, competition, push me and lift me above myself. And unison is an altogether boring quality in discussion.
>
> As our mind is strengthened by communication with vigorous and orderly minds, so it is impossible to say how much it loses and degenerates by our continual association and frequentation with mean and sickly minds. There is no contagion that spreads like that one. . . .
>
> I enter into discussion and argument with great freedom and ease, inasmuch as opinion finds in me a bad soil to penetrate and take deep roots in. No propositions astonish me, no belief offends me, whatever contrast it offers with my own. . . .
>
> When someone opposes me, he arouses my attention, not my anger. I go tó meet a man who contradicts me, who instructs me. The cause of truth should be common cause for both. . . .
> (Montaigne:704–05)

Montaigne points to the delight of the shared practice of mutually seeking for truth in agonistic (not uncommitted, neutral, academic) conversation. This practice requires no external epistemic foundation; convincing people to participate in it, if conviction is necessary, requires practical work and prudential arguments. Modern versions of this practice appear as the "unconstrained communication" postulated by Habermas, the "conversation" advocated by Rorty, and the "universal solidarity" championed by Welch (1990). Beyond the posturing of polemics, such approaches offer the possibility of reasonable and humane argument without a false presumption of the disputants' uncommitted neutrality.

Engaging in such a conversation is an appropriate practice for philosophers of religion (and others) who seek both to understand religious practice and to discern whether any specific practice is preferable in a situation of diversity in practices and conflict over ultimate beliefs. I will argue in chapter 5 that the more a religious tradition (and its institutions and communities) is committed to the pursuit of wisdom, to "the common cause of truth," in Montaigne's words, the wiser it is for people to be committed to such a tradition and its practices. But that is to anticipate the end of the argument, while we are near the beginning.

But by most accounts from the mainstream of philosophy of religion, such a view is hardly in the line of Montaigne or Blaise

Pascal, who sought to write an apology for Christianity that would undermine the religious indifference characteristic of his own time. They are "fideists" who, by definition, are skeptical about rational foundations for faith or even, perhaps, of the reasonableness of "deciding" for faith. These internalists allegedly resolve the problem, suggests Penelhum (1983:71), by recommending conformity to avoid commitment (Montaigne) or to induce it (Pascal). Although Pascal's famous Wager is acknowledged to be an argument of sorts, it is not an appeal to reason, but to "prudential self-interest." Although Penelhum calls it "irrefutable" given Pascal's assumptions (71), we cannot give him those assumptions without making a fideistic choice. Or so philosophers often claim. But, in fact, the Wager is a very subtle, practical argument which points a way to finding a wise commitment. Its force can be seen when one has a practical, rather than an academic and doctrinal, understanding of religion.

PASCAL'S WAGER AND RELIGIOUS PRACTICE

The Wager argument is so well known as to need little exposition. First, the Wager is unavoidable: God is or God is not, and your life declares which bet you make. You cannot avoid wagering since you are already *in medias res*. We are all like the stranded mountaineer in James's "The Will to Believe" (1896); we must choose either to follow the path that may be useless or remain where we are and likely die quietly. Second, the Wager involves specifiable risks and benefits. If you do believe in God, and if there is no God, you may have a finite and temporal loss (perhaps the goods obtained in immoral practices from which you abstain, although this loss might be balanced by the goods that religious practices brings). If you don't believe in God, and if there is no God, you gain some finite temporal goods, which you might have lost had you abstained from practices incompatible with belief. If you do believe in God, and if there is a God, your gain is an "eternity of life and happiness." If you don't believe in God, and if there is a God, you may have a temporal and finite gain, but you miss out on an infinite gain. Therefore, since the risks are equal, and the benefits infinitely disproportionate, the wise person will bet on God, for the benefits of that risk infinitely outweigh the benefits of the other risk. On many accounts, here ends the argument.

The Wager has recently been defended by Lycan and Schlesinger (1989) and by Morris (1986b; 1992). Morris notes that Pascal's Wager is not an "epistemically unconcerned project" (Morris 1986b:261). The wagerer finds both belief and unbelief relatively on an epistemic par with each other: both make roughly equal appeal and both seem to have roughly equal support. In this context, most standard objections to the Wager vanish. As Morris put it:

> It is not an assumption of the Wager that God will reward a person for a deliberate, calculated charade of belief undertaken and maintained on the grounds of the grossest self-interest. So the famous objection of William James, who was offended by such an assumption, misses the point (Morris 1986b:267).[7]

Nor does the Wager require a threat of punishment or promise of reward from God. As Morris notes, the text requires neither. Once one realizes the situation of the wagerer (as the dominant strand in modern philosophy of religion with its academic bias does not), most of the alleged problems with the Wager argument drop out.

The problem that remains, however, is that the epistemically concerned subject who wagers has not two options, but many. Our choices are not between theism and atheism, but between atheism and the many gods proposed by the various religious traditions. Given that there are a large number of possibilities, and given that the wager is constructed assuming an "either-or" situation, the Wager therefore seems substantially flawed. Penelhum has well described this possibility (1983:73–74).

In one sense, however, the "many gods" problem may be rationally solvable by using Anselm's definition of God as "that than which a greater cannot be conceived" as Lycan and Schlesinger point out (1989:275–78). The Wager requires not that one choose a god to one's taste, but that the God which one chooses must be the greater than any other, for this God and only this God holds out the possibility of the greatest (infinite) gain. Worship of any other god would be like participating in a practice with finite benefit. Thus, if one has a "choice" among deities, and one cannot worship them all, worshiping that than which a greater cannot be conceived offers one the greatest possible benefit. Devotion to the "other gods" is or entails disbelief in that than which a greater cannot be conceived. Therefore, the assumption of the Wager is not necessarily a fideistic choice. It can be construed as a forced option: either believe in that than which a greater cannot be conceived or believe in anything else. But only one belief has the possibility of infinite gain. So the wise person will choose that faith over any other. The problem of "many gods" does not defeat the wager.

Alas, that may not solve the problem because the problem is a practical one. Many traditions are constituted by radically different practices for worshiping that than which a greater cannot be conceived. Taking the problem of religious diversity as a problem of "many Gods" centers on the doctrine of God. But this doctrine is not the real problem. Indeed, this interpretation is the wrong approach because it leaves the real, practical problem intact—*how to* devote oneself to the Infinite. The presumptions of modern philosophy that religious belief is an individual's disposition or property rather than a practice leaves the practical problem of "many gods" unresolved.

There is a practical way around this practical problem. One must see clearly the situation in which the Wager comes into play. Two factors relevant to the force of the Wager are rarely considered. Yet these alone show how the Wager can help resolve the practical problem, at least for people in specific circumstances.

First, it is important to know the purposes for which Pascal composed the argument and people it was intended to convince. All too often, the wager argument is taken as a neutral and purely philosophical argument, a rhetorical move in a polite conversation carried on by unconcerned academics in professional journals. If one has such a presumption, as Morris suggests, one cannot understand how the Wager could work as a practical argument. Terence Penelhum (1983) provides a description of the addressees to whom the *Apology* (of which *Pensées* as we have them are fragments) was to have been issued:

> The *Apology* was [to be] addressed primarily to Pascal's cultivated and freethinking contemporaries, who were assumed to be interested in the dramatic developments in the natural sciences and their implications, to possess some degree of philosophical sophistication and to have been wearied by the bitter religious divisions that had plunged France into civil warfare. Such an audience would have acquired an inclination toward skepticism, and to a self-protective and superficial religious conformity. For such people the writings of Montaigne would have been a major influence, and it is clearly Montaigne from whom Pascal derives his understanding of Skepticism. Pascal is passionately convinced that neither the noble pretensions of rationalist philosophies, be they Stoic or Cartesian, nor the easy-going Conformism

of Montaigne can offer man an appropriate antidote to anxiety. And the faith which alone can save them is a passionate surrender of the whole personality. . . . (Penelhum 1983:62–63)

Pascal's situation is like that described by Montaigne (and, I would add, like that which obtains in the present "secularized" context): religious camps have been at war with each other with dreadful consequences not only for individual believers, but also for both churches and the state. One upshot of their disagreement is that the starry skies above no longer show the splendor of God; the book of nature no longer unambiguously reveals its Author to these jaded unbelievers.

The *purpose* of Pascal's argument, and centrally of the Wager, is not to complete an academic quest for truth, but to bring persons to accept the truth of religious faith and practice. The way for them to solve their problem in a situation of uncertainty is not to engage in more philosophical argument, but in taking up a practice in which they learn *how* to see, *how* to read. Abstracting the argument and its purpose from its specific addressees in their social context, especially if one takes it to be an academic argument, easily distorts it and undermines its force. In its own context, the Wager may be an apologetic argument, but that does not make it unphilosophical. Its philosophical force is generally to point its hearers away from pure, abstract, mental theory to dirty, messy, bodily practice.

The second factor is the connection of Pascal's well-known final remedy of "masses and holy water" to the Wager. If one sees the Wager argument as ending with the big bet, then this point seems unimportant. And if it is important, Pascal's advocacy of this specific remedy may, *in the context of religious animosity*, simply beg the practical question by presuming an answer to what is really at issue. Why *this* practice in *this* religious tradition rather than some other? Huguenots and Catholics have been killing each other, in part to establish whether even an attenuated form of religious tolerance is to be permitted in France or in specific *departments*. Not only are these disputants epistemically committed, they also have political and religious commitments. Doesn't Pascal's remedy beg the practical question in favor of the Catholics?

A close reading of some *Pensées* suggests he might not. In *Pensées*, Pascal's imagined interlocutor *admits the force* of the first part of the Wager argument. The interlocutor then continues and Pascal responds:

"I am forced to wager, and am not free. I am not released, and am so made that I cannot believe. What, then, would you have me do?"

True. But at least learn your inability to believe, since reason brings you to this, and yet you cannot believe. Endeavor then to convince yourself, not by increase of proofs of God, but by the abatement of your passions. You would like to attain faith, and do not know the way; you would like to cure yourself of unbelief and ask the remedy for it. Learn of those who have been bound like you, and who are cured of an ill of which you would be cured. Follow the way by which they began; by acting as if they believed, taking the holy water, having masses said, etc. Even this will naturally make you believe, and deaden your acuteness.—"But this is what I am afraid of."—And why? What have you to lose?

But to show you that this leads you there, it is this which will lessen the passions, which are your stumbling blocks.

The end of this discourse.—Now what harm will befall you in taking this side? You will be faithful, honest, humble, grateful, generous, a sincere friend, truthful. Certainly you will not have those poisonous pleasures, glory and luxury; but will you not have others? I will tell you that you will thereby gain in this life, and that, at each step you take on this road, you will see so great certainty of gain, so much nothingness in what you risk, that you will at last recognize that you have wagered for something certain and infinite, for which you have given nothing.

"Ah! This discourse transports me, charms me," etc.

If this discourse pleases you and seems impressive, know that it is made by a man who has knelt, both before and after it, in prayer to that Being, infinite and without parts, before whom he lays all he has, for you also to lay before Him all you have for your own good and for His glory, that so strength may be given to lowliness (Pascal:§233).

This specific section presents the practical component of the wager. It is exceedingly rich and its various parts need to be unpacked.

First, Pascal has a psychological diagnosis of the interlocutor's unbelief: his passion is getting in the way of his reason. The interlocutor accepts the cogency of the argument. Having done so, how can the interlocutor *not* believe? The problem cannot be intellectual; thus, it must be passional. The interlocutor's "acuteness" is not intellectual, but passional, scruple.

Second, Pascal has a therapy for the interlocutor. Pascal is certainly not presuming that our beliefs are fully within our control. His therapy is indirect; it does not directly give the interlocutor a belief or require an act of will that will create a belief. Instead, Pascal pre-scribes a specific set of practices which, properly and dutifully under-taken, will likely bring about belief. Presumably, the interlocutor's practices have not led to religion; but vicious practices have given one a taste for poisonous pleasures. These practices shape character and obstruct the intellect and get in the way of one's accepting religion. If, however, the interlocuter will give up the practices of seeking glory and wealth and take up the religious practices of seeking God, he or she can become a person who can develop a taste for the satisfactions religious practices bring, especially a taste for communion with God. And one who engages in practical religion will naturally develop beliefs about God and God's worshipfulness. The Wager argument, to which the interlocutor has "notionally" assented, will come to full fruition in practice and enable "real" assent (to use John Henry Newman's terms) not because more arguments pile up, but because the interlocuter will become, through engaging in religious practices, a rather different person. Having participated in those practices, such a one will become a person who can be awestruck by *les espaces infinis* and see through the book of nature to the Mind that wrote it. Such a one will become a person of faith whom God graces, not a devotee of poisonous pleasures.

Third, although the "presenting complaint" of the heartsick in-terlocutor is intellectual, the real problem is a hidden disease of the passions. Pascal prescribes a set of practices that will not merely bring about external conformity (as James may have thought) or contrived faith, but will reshape the interlocutor's desires so that the religious life and the rewards it promises becomes desirable. One's character will acquire the shape that will make an infinite gain be no mere compensation for conformity, but an appropriate satisfaction growing out of and properly crowning a life of truly religious practice.

Fourth, and finally, the Wager Argument is not a monologic demonstration, but an implicit dialogue. Engaging in the Wager is not here portrayed as an isolated individual's privately betting his life. Rather, the Wager is a shared practice, a conversational remedy in which more than one voice is needed.

However, given the conflicted context, Pascal's therapeutic an-swer at this point in *Pensées* does indeed seem to beg the practical question badly. But part of the social context and thus the conditions in which religious indifference, conformity, and skepticism is a live option is the multiplicity of competing traditions and practices. Pascal here simply presumes that Catholic practices will properly bring the interlocutor to be the sort of person who can accept religious belief in a real, not notional, way. In a situation in which practitioners vilify each others' paths, no practices may seem attractive. Why prefer to take up this practice or set of practices rather than another? Pascal seems to ignore this question here.

Two further themes, however, suggest a resolution of this practical problem. First, Pascal uses considerable space to argue that *"the true Jews and the true Christians have but the same religion"*(§609). Although Judaism seemed to consist in external practices, true Jews practiced the same religion as the true Christians: "the love of God"(§609). Pascal works hard to distinguish the carnal from the spiritual in discussing the figures and types found in the Old Testament. The upshot of these meditations is that Pascal suggests that true religion is not found as much in the institution, community, or tradition to which one is attached, as in the way religion is practiced and the sort of God to which the practice is devoted. Combining these points with the noetic solution to the "many gods" problem, we can say that good religious practices may be found in more than one religion if the intentional object of those practices is that than which a greater cannot be conceived.[8]

Second, Pascal does give some (rather weak and, by present standards, uninformed) arguments against Islam and the religions of China. But his point here is to argue that some religions are inferior to Judaism and Christianity:

> I see then a crowd of religions in many parts of the world and in all times; but their morality cannot please me, nor could their proofs convince me. Thus I should equally have rejected the religion of Mahomet and of China, of ancient Romans and of the Egyptians, for the sole reason, that none having more marks of truth than another, nor anything which should necessarily persuade me, reason cannot incline to one rather than the other (§618).

In William James's (1896) terms, these are not "live options" for Pascal. They do not even qualify to enter the race, much less to have a chance to be the subject of a wager.

Here is the shape, then, of the practical religious epistemology exemplified by Pascal. The situation is this: true heathenism (religious indifference, moral laxity, love of the carnal) and true religion (as evinced in authentic Jewish and Christian practice of the love of that than which a greater cannot be conceived) are options on a relative epistemic par for engaged epistemic subjects. Pascal, like us, is not an epistemically unconcerned subject. His intellect is no religious *tabula rasa*. He is a situated subject who has reduced the religious options to two—finite and infinite, worldly and spiritual devotion. The question is which path to take.

Here then is the real problem of religious diversity. It needs to be solved not by "simple conformity" or by a retreat to abstraction. The solution begins with an acknowledgment that the problem is a situated one. Embodied persons struggling with practical issues acknowledge the authoritative patterns of practices that appeal for their commitment. That the disembodied academic mind can toy with other patterns is fine, but irrelevant. The real problem is one of commitment and the wager is the wager of life. While the academic mind may investigate unappealing practices and construct theoretical arguments, the person in which that mind is embodied makes the wager, not as much by isolated investigations, as by a pattern of commitments to practices. In short, Pascal's Wager argument suggests that we can construe the tradition of Montaigne and Pascal, not as "internalist" and "fideist," but as practical. They show how to engage in the practice of engaged conversation about wise religious practice in a conflicted situation and thereby come to a practical resolution of real religious problems.

But to advocate finding a viable alternative to the fading modern, individualistic, academic, externalist practice of religious epistemology is not to advocate that one make a fideistic choice or leap of faith, nor to suggest that we need merely retrieve Pascal's arguments. Rather, the alternative is to engage in developing a practical religious epistemology, to take up the shared practice of seeking the wisdom of a religious commitment, and to enter into one of the shared religious practices of committed seeking valorized by Pascal in the wake of Montaigne.

This practical tradition points the way beyond internalism and externalism in modern philosophy of religion. The burning religious question is a practical question—an ethical one in the broad sense. The issues involved in exploring the ethics of belief are practical ones: Since practices shape us as persons, into which practices shall we place or continue to place our bodies, our minds, ourselves? To answer this question we need to go beyond the dominant pattern in modern philosophy of religion. A practical religious epistemology is the discipline to which we submit to answer that question.

Yet one of the key problems with modern philosophy of religion in general, as mentioned in the first sections of this chapter, is its "presumption of substitutability," the idea that validating or upending the propositions that express religious beliefs can settle the issue about religion. Like epistemology more generally, religious epistemology has been impractical. It implicitly either equates religion with religious belief or finds that examining religious belief is sufficient for examining religion. The following chapter shows that religion is not mere belief by presenting a practical, working definition of religion. Chapter 3 then shows that validating propositions which are the content of religious beliefs cannot stand in for the engaged examination of religion in practice.

NOTES TO CHAPTER 1

1. The evident exception is D. Z. Phillips who has bucked the mainstream in philosophy of religion by espousing a Wittgensteinian approach that makes the religious form of life central. But Phillips's approach leaves no room to ask whether anyone *ought* to participate in a religious form of life or in which religious form of life one should participate, which is precisely the issue in the tradition of Montaigne and Pascal that is presented in this chapter. As the reign of modernity has waned, philosophers of religion have begun to take new paths in understanding religion, for example, cross-cultural comparative philosophy of religion (Hick 1989) and studies of the coherence of traditional theological doctrines (Morris 1986a).

2. The evident exception is Alston (1991) some of whose accomplishments I note in the next chapter. However, Alston does not adequately recognize the variety of religious practices and I do not see how his predominantly externalist epistemological stance can deal with issues raised by Code (1991) and Jaggar (1989) among others and their significance for religious practice.

3. I have sketched this situation in a slightly later period as a problem of many authorities (see Tilley 1991:221–225, and the literature cited there). Toulmin (1992) has discussed the social history of France in the late sixteenth and early seventeenth century and shown how the arguments about religion were not leisurely notional arguments, but urgent practical ones.

4. I use *phronesis* here rather than "prudence" because prudence has become associated in much modern philosophy not with the practical wisdom Aristotle described, but with cost-benefit or risk-benefit calculations, often self-serving ones. In general, I will use terms like "wisdom" or "practical wisdom" as English equivalents for *phronesis*.

5. 'Epistemologists' is here in scare quotes to note the fact that there is an ongoing dispute about the possibility of a feminist epistemology. See Code 1991:314–324 for a discussion of this issue.

6. This usage should not be confused with "internalism" and "externalism" in epistemology, which comes to the fore in chapter 3. The epistemic externalist finds that a believer may have a justified or warranted belief without being aware of how or being able to show that that belief is justified or warranted. The epistemic internalist includes such awareness in some way as a necessary condition for knowing, warrant, or justification.

7. Philosophical commentary on the Wager argument has usually taken the issue Pascal addresses to be theoretical, not practical. James (1896) wrongly presumes that one must antecedently have faith in the practice to undertake it: "A faith in masses and holy water adopted wilfully after such a mechanical calculation would lack the inner soul of faith's reality" (6). Morris's criticism is on target, but James is correct in one thing: he takes the problem of "many *practices*" (which I develop below) seriously, while Morris (1992), working out of a committed Christian perspective, ignores this possibility. One cannot have faith in masses and holy water antecedent to participating in the practice; one participates and develops faith in and love of God through participating seriously in the practices. The real issue, then, is practical: which practices, which set of practices, should be ours when more than one set is open to us? So far as I know, Morris has not followed Pascal into Catholic practices, and seems not even to have considered the question of intra-Christian pluralism seriously, an issue whose acuteness will become clear in the final section of chapter 3.

8. Jonathan Wilson, in correspondence, suggests that this approach may lead to a liberal, pluralistic account construing each religion as a particular and partial response to a transcendent One. But what makes soteriocentric pluralism (see Hick 1989 or Knitter 1985) an attractive option is that it is an improvement over inclusivist and exclusivist views of salvation. The present approach is not soteriocentric and does not address, much less start with, problems of salvation. I don't think one can theoretically resolve such problems as who is saved or whether all religions are different responses to the One. Nor do I think response to the Greatest or the One is a foundation for religious belief. It is a constituent of some religious practices, this Anselmian twist on Pascal merely rules out some practices and some traditions as embodying wise religious commitment. It is not a foundation for belief.

2

Religion Practically Defined

Anthropologists, sociologists, psychologists, phenomenologists, and even theologians who study religion academically have shown that understanding religion requires more than understanding religious beliefs abstracted from religious life. Hence, when philosophers of religion examine religious propositions apart from their home in religious life, they wring the text from its context. They run the danger of constructing a "rational theology" that simply defends the entitlement of a disembodied mind with no social location to hold certain propositions about God or the Ultimate. But such defense has little, if any, connection with practical issues.

The purpose of this chapter is to develop a practical working definition of religion. I will not defend this procedure a priori, but allow the exposition to speak for itself and meet specific objections along the way. Nonetheless, two preliminary remarks are in order.

First, the definition of religion used here does not focus on individual religious participants or their beliefs. The reason for this is simple: Religion is essentially social. Save (possibly) for the founders of religions who create new forms of religious life out of the traditions they inherit, religious people derive their religion from participation in (including, for some, the process of conversion to) a tradition. Although the beliefs and practices of innovative individuals are often of great interest, as William James showed in *The Varieties of Religious Experience* (1902), even James's most original subjects derived their central beliefs and practices from the traditions in which they participated, however much they reformed or revolutionized their traditions.[1]

Second, once one advocates a practical approach that attends to social locations, one can no longer write as if one were a free-floating academic mind seeking to show that "anyone" might be warranted or justified in holding a single belief. The presumptions that undergird the grand academic style purporting to find "what all of us rational

29

men [*sic*] do rationally believe or can be rationally persuaded to believe" are no longer tenable. Authors are not innocent of interests, although they may be aware enough of their interests not to lose control of their ideas.

Unlike most major Anglo-American writers in philosophy of religion, I am not Protestant in background, but Catholic; not conservative, but progressive; not fixed in my religious (or antireligious) practices and views, but open to change. Like most, I am a university professor, and part of the familiar contingent of overweight, married, heterosexual, middle-class, white males. My politics are left-liberal, my social attitudes radically egalitarian and rather tolerant, my religious disposition fundamentally anticlericalist, my religious practice regular, but not obsessive. Such a cliché-ridden sketch of my social location fails, no doubt, to reveal all my relevant biases and interests, but it may help to locate some of the practical and theoretical choices I have made, some of the examples I use, and some of my differences from the mainstream of contemporary philosophy of religion.

THE PRACTICAL THEORY OF RELIGION RENEWED

McClendon (1994) supports what he calls a "practical" theory of religion. He portrays this theory in the following:

> A religion is a set of powerful *practices* that embody the life-forming convictions of its practitioners. There *is* no 'essence' of religion; religions are neither . . . all more or less true nor . . . all more or less evil. It follows that generalizations about religion are generally mistaken, since religions differ in kind, and only concrete, sympathetic historical and empirical study can tell us about any particular religion. We may call this the *practical theory* of religion . . . in the sense that its concern is the life-shaping (as I will say, the convictional) *practices* religions embody. So religions are not to be identified with their abstract teachings, far less with their 'errors.' . . . (421).

In McClendon's usage, "practice" is a technical term, akin to Alasdair MacIntyre's understanding of "practice."[2] McClendon writes:

> Social practices, like games, strive for some end beyond themselves (health for the practice of medicine, livable space for architecture), require intentional participation on the part of practitioners, employ determinate means, and proceed according to

rules. As there, a "practice" . . . is a complex series of human actions involving definite practitioners who by these means and in accordance with these rules together seek the understood end (28).

McClendon's work can be seen as a useful contemporary version of the "practical" tradition in understanding religion characterized in the first chapter.

Yet McClendon's claim that "generalizations about religion are generally mistaken" must be nuanced. In one sense it is clearly true: it is untenable to claim that a defining characteristic marks off religions from other forms of human activity. For every "defining characteristic" one scholar finds, other scholars either point out that there is a tradition which is clearly a religion which does not have it or highlight a tradition or practice which has that characteristic, but clearly is not a religion. Nor can one assume from the presence of a concept or practice in one tradition that another tradition has that sort of concept or practice. McClendon is right to claim that there is no "essence" of religion or any generally accepted formal definition of religion.

Yet to say that we cannot treat religion as a group of shared human activities with a set of family resemblances and thus develop a practical working definition does not follow from McClendon's claim. A working definition is open to exceptions: There may well be a religion it doesn't fit or some movement or institution or tradition that it does fit which isn't (at least obviously) religious. There are "gray areas" on the margins. But a working definition of "religion" helpfully highlights the core of the contested concept to show what it is that religionists study, what it is for a person to participate in a religion. A working definition is always *pro tempore*, and subject to correction. A religion is a tradition, that is, a set of practices composed of specific patterns of actions, beliefs and dispositions (attitudes, feelings). Specifically, it

- usually takes a set of (oral or written) texts as in some way normative;
- has participants who are or try to be followers of a founder, model, or archetypal figure or of a path created or discovered by such a figure;
- holds out a final goal or ultimate blessing for the participants (and sometimes for all humanity); and

- is passed on through local communities that are embedded in enduring institutions.

The next task is to explicate this working definition and show how philosophers of religion err if they abstract religious beliefs as the only part of religion worth examination.

RELIGION AS A TRADITION

A religion is a tradition, a set of practices composed of specific patterns of acting, believing, and feeling. The elements of such practices are so woven together that they can be distinguished analytically but not separated practically. Specific beliefs can function as presumptions or frameworks for ritual practices, as when Roman Catholics believe in the real presence of Christ in the bread and wine of the Eucharist. Such a belief undergirds the properly devout Catholic's attitudes not only toward the Eucharist and the way the eucharistic elements are to be handled in a ritual setting, but also toward oneself as a participant in the ritual. The ritual practice can function to reinforce beliefs and attitudes, as when during the Mass the priest engages in gestures highlighting the consecration of the bread and wine that reinforce belief in the Real Presence and evoke an attitude of reverence. The attitudes one has can strengthen the beliefs and may be necessary for a proper participation in a ritual.

Religious traditions have been helpfully understood as "cultural-symbolic systems" (Geertz), "discourse practices" (Boone), and "semiotic systems" in which semantic, syntactic, and pragmatic components are interrelated (Schreiter). Because there are such tight connections between religious actions, beliefs, and attitudes, one cannot understand religious beliefs without understanding the other components. Thus, the meaning of the doctrine of the Real Presence can be paraphrased or summarized theologically, but cannot be fully understood except when it is connected with the ritual practices of the community that holds the doctrine.[3] As Schreiter has pointed out, changes in the ritual practices of the Roman Catholic tradition, for example, Mass celebrated in the vernacular with the presider facing the people rather than in Latin with the priest facing the wall or "leading the people," significantly affected the belief in the Real Presence in the religious life of Catholics. Theologians still working with the same theological concepts and verbally unchanged doctrinal abstractions may not have noticed any shift, despite the shift in ritual. In fact, the meaning of the doctrine of the Real Presence can shift significantly, when the practices with which it is connected change.

The classic theological dilemma here is whether a missionary can and ought use the proposition that Christ is really present in the eucharistic elements to evangelize a tribe that has a tradition of practicing ritual cannibalism. The philosophical point is not how to resolve the problem, but that the problem arises. The dilemma suggests that a proposition may have significantly different religious meanings in the different religious and nonreligious practices in which it is used. When philosophers abstract a proposition for discussion, they place it in another practice. Given that the propositions they deal with are actually ingredient in religious practices, philosophers, as much as missionaries, need to recognize the problems of meaning shifts. Alas, most philosophers of religion seem to take for granted that when they discuss a proposition abstracted from a belief ensconced in a religious practice, the proposition they discuss has the same meaning as it had in the religious practice. But this meaning cannot always be taken for granted.

When philosophers examine religious beliefs, they typically focus on belief in God and its justifiability. Yet certainly the reasonableness of holding a single proposition, "there is a God," is too abstract to determine the reasonableness of being religious or of participating in a religious tradition. According to public opinion polls, more than 90 percent of the American populace believes in God; yet fewer than half of them are regular participants in worship (Woodward 1993:80). Even if all of those who believe in God were rationally warranted in doing so, such a belief is so nominal for so many that it has nothing to do with religious practices and attitudes.[4] The absence of a necessary connection between propositional beliefs and religious practice means that the examination of an individual's entitlement to hold a proposition such as "God is speaking to me now" (see Plantinga 1981) cannot suffice for understanding the wisdom of commitment to and participation in a religious tradition. Such examination may tell us something about an abstract "typical" individual's rationality, but tells us next to nothing about the religious tradition, if any, in which that individual participates or the wisdom of any actual person's participation.[5]

Philosophers of religion often try to escape this problem by stipulating that they are presuming the "traditional" doctrine of God in Christianity. That is, they assume they are dealing with a central and distinctive doctrine of the tradition when they work with a specific proposition. Showing that one is not irrational in accepting this proposition or that one is entitled to believe it would then make it plausible that people who participate in the tradition are reasonable. However, that approach not only sunders the connections between the doctrine and the tradition, it also has another serious problem: the traditional central claim of Christianity about God is that God is triune; the god of the philosophers is not clearly so.

Although philosophers have examined the logic of trinitarian doctrines, they rarely invoke a trinitarian concept of God in other contexts. As often as not, the God of whom philosophers write may as well be unitarian as trinitarian.[6] This is one aspect of Pascal's distinction of the God of the philosophers from the God of Abraham, Isaac, and Jacob. Philosophers' concepts of God are not clearly the concepts of God found in specific religious traditions and connected to other beliefs, dispositions, and practices.

Further, it is not clear that the philosophers' concept of God "as classically understood" is a central *and distinctive* part of any specific religious tradition. Certainly, western monotheisms have typically held belief in God as central. But one can be an observant Jew without significant belief in God, and perhaps without any serious commitment to monotheism. Moreover, pure monotheistic belief does not necessarily distinguish Islam from monotheistic Judaism. Even if belief in the Trinity is sufficiently different to be a central and distinctive belief of most Christians, that belief still does not distinguish Anglo-Catholicism from Missouri Synod Lutheranism. This failure to distinguish "denominations" may seem an irrelevant point. However, the fact that it is taken as irrelevant is precisely the problem. As I will argue in chapter 3 failure to make such a distinction undermines one recent exemplary attempt to escape the problem of vagueness, an attempt in which the residual Pascalian problem of "many practices" appears in a different key.

Within a religious tradition, a set of central and distinctive beliefs coinheres with a web of prescribed and proscribed patterns of actions and attitudes. In that sense, to understand a given belief, action, or attitude, one has to understand where it fits within the interleaved web and which other elements of the web are relevant to determining its meaning. Abstracting it from the web for purposes of analysis is surely legitimate. But asking whether a person is entitled to believe a proposition *p* without regard to its connections with the rest of the web in which it is imbedded sunders those connections. Thus, showing that one is entitled to hold a proposition such as "God exists" says little or nothing about religious belief in God.

In sum, the central and distinctive convictions of a tradition can be summarized in a creed, narrated in a myth, or explored in a theological treatise, etc. But in the life of a religion, proclaiming a creed, narrating a myth, exploring a doctrine are practices connected with other practices. To understand the significance of those beliefs, one needs to know how they are contextualized in the practices and attitudes that constitute the tradition.

Traditions prescribe and proscribe some actions and practices. What must I do to be a good or true Buddhist or Baptist? How can I live as a left-handed Tantrist or a Sivite? Even if religious traditions do not do so, academics tend to divide the answers to such questions into the areas of morality and ritual.

Members of a tradition ordinarily participate in its ritual practices. A tradition may carry and be carried by life-cycle rituals, practices undertaken at the key transitions in life from birth to death. Calendar rituals may be performed on a weekly, monthly, or annual basis as ways of marking and dedicating the life of the individual and community. There may be crisis rituals designed to dedicate oneself or to implore the mercy of the powers that be in times of unexpected crisis from famine to war. Even the most austere religious traditions incorporate rituals—one suspects that they are identified as "austere" traditions simply because their rituals are minimal or latent rather than fulsome and patent. Learning how to participate in such rituals is one way in which a person develops the beliefs and attitudes the tradition carries.

Members of a tradition ordinarily perform specific acts and avoid other acts. One may have to avoid specific people and places. One must work to develop in oneself and others specific character traits. No good Southern Baptist could frequent a house of prostitution. No good Theravadin monk could seek employment as a butcher. In Judaism, Torah gives mitzvot. According to Maimonides, there are 248 positive commandments and 365 negative ones. All of these moral and ritual practices with their prescriptions and proscriptions form a constituent part of each tradition. They also shape the specific doctrine of God in the theistic traditions or the way to "ultimate release" or "extinction" in nontheistic traditions.

When examining a religious tradition, one cannot neglect its moral component. When examining a religious doctrine, one cannot neglect the practices to which it is properly or necessarily connected.

Even if one does not entirely accept Max Weber's *The Protestant Ethic and the Spirit of Capitalism* (1959), one sees therein the links between belief and practice in that part of the Christian tradition. Even if one does not accept all feminist critiques of the Christian traditions, feminists have clearly shown that Christianity is not immune to sexism and has at times encouraged the subjugation of women. Recognizing and understanding such links between moral practices and beliefs are essential for understanding the religious tradition as it is embodied.

Although it has become a commonplace that there is no such thing as "religious language," but only language used in religious contexts, there is a nexus of analogous issues that generally form a central focus for a religious tradition. What makes these issues "religious" is not merely their content but the fact that their meaning is in part constituted by their being ingredients in the pattern of practices which constitute a tradition.

First, one finds a focus on the origins and the destiny of everything. The tradition provides answers to ultimate questions. Where did we come from? Where are we going? The virulent debate between "evolutionists" and "creationists" indicates the centrality of issues concerned with origins and destinies. But nonreligious traditions, for example, secular humanism, also answer such questions. Indeed, the similarities in attitude and content between one of the classic expressions of that tradition, Bertrand Russell's *The Free Man's Worship*, and some forms of Theravada Buddhist and Vedantic Hindu asceticism can be seen (though the differences in practice are even more marked). What makes the religious traditions identifiably religious and Russell's humanism only quasi-religious at best is that there is little family resemblance between the patterns of practices even though specific beliefs, attitudes, and actions are present in both religious and nonreligious traditions. More specifically, the absence of prescribed or commonly accepted birth rites, propitiatory rites, and burial rites in secular humanism seems to break the pattern. Roughly, in most religious traditions such attitudes and beliefs are intrinsically connected to ritual life; in secular humanism they are not.

Second, one finds a focus on the way things go right and the way things go wrong in the world. Why is there so much suffering? Why is there so much evil? Religious traditions will provide answers and inculcate "theodicies" (in Berger's sense). Sometimes religious traditions legitimate established social orders. In other contexts, religions challenge or deny the legitimacy of established social structures. Again, nonreligious traditions, such as many forms of Marxism, answer such questions. Yet religious "answers" are again intrinsically connected with identifiable attitudes and ritual practices, whereas nonreligious answers are not so clearly intrinsically linked (although at least some forms of Communism land in the "gray area" as possibly indistinguishable in practice from the clearly religious traditions; see Bowker 1970:137–192).

Third, one finds a focus on the ways that what is wrong with the world are to be set right. In many traditions, the righting of the social world involves participating in ritual acts and following moral norms in ways so intimately connected that the modern distinction between ritual and morality is dissolved. The linking of Confucian concepts of *te* (virtue, charisma) and *li* (propriety, ritual) exemplifies this connection. Examining almost any of the various Buddhist traditions' understandings of how to walk the Holy Eightfold Path will also show the purely nominal and theoretical nature of such distinctions, at least from their perspectives. The solution to worldly woes may be possible only through practices that many westerners arbitrarily divide into fields of ritual and morality.

Fourth, one finds a focus on attitudes about oneself, one's family, one's community, one's society, and one's world inscribed in these traditions. Religions tend to inculcate overarching attitudes toward the whole world and each of the human spheres (personal, interpersonal, familial, communal, tribal, organizational, national, natural) within it. The world may be nothing but *maya*, as the Rig Veda has it. With such an attitude, various practices for penetrating the veil of illusion or understanding the manifoldness of everything or seeing the Dancer in the dancing can be prescribed. Or the world may be a garden created by a god for us to live in. If so, then tending the garden is the proper attitude for getting on with our lives. Attitudes make a difference about how one lives: dancing is not gardening.

Often philosophers overlook the importance of such attitudes and collapse them into merely cognitive beliefs. But that won't do. For instance, some Christians have said that one can't be a Christian until one realizes one is a sinner. One has to *take oneself to be* a sinner. This realization is not merely a belief one holds true. It involves an important attitude to all of one's life. It is not a "nominal" belief, whose meaning can be captured in a bare proposition, but a conviction that shapes one's life; to realize the significance of this conviction requires learning how to be a sinner, and how to realize redemption. Some Buddhists seek Enlightenment as the goal of life. Enlightenment is not only a belief about what the goal of life is or ought to be, but involves a very complex attitude that is neither grasping desire for Enlightenment nor indifference to Enlightenment nor the construal of Enlightenment as an individual achievement. One cannot take credit for Enlightenment nor regard it as a gratuitous gift that one may or may not accept. The full range of human emotions and attitudes from fear to trust, hope to despair, empowerment to powerlessness, joy to sorrow, wondering awe to disdain can be found in the religious traditions.

Generally speaking, religions are conservative or preservative, but they are not necessarily unchangeably rigid. As traditions, religions tend to preserve rather than analyze the practical pattern of beliefs, dispositions, and actions that constitute the tradition. But such "traditionalism" does not imply that some religions are not reformist or cannot be reformed. Religions are often reformed. Jesus began as a reformer of Judaism; Buddha, as a reformer of Hinduism. Within traditions specific people often play roles that explore and expand the tradition simply as a way to keep a tradition vibrant (cf. von Hügel 1904).

Nor does religious traditionalism imply that religions must be politically or socially conservative. Reform and revolution can be a religious pattern, as shown by the sixteenth-century revolution of Puritan saints, the Christian socialist activism in nineteenth-century Britain, the varied contemporary forms of liberation theology, the nonviolent practices of Gandhi and other reform movements. What makes religions potentially revolutionary is their attempt to spread and preserve the tradition in a social environment whose practices ignore or oppose those of the religious tradition.

Understanding religion, then, begins with recognizing that it is a tradition, a set of practices with interlinked specific patterns of actions, beliefs, and dispositions. One rather common feature of religious traditions is the practice of transmitting texts (whether orally or in writing). If one is a Buddhist, one will know stories of Gautama the Buddha and of Enlightenment; if one is a modern Hindu, one may revere the *Bhagavad Gita*; if one is a Jew one will know the stories of the Exodus and may allow the commandments, which are part of that narrative and the ongoing story of Judaism, to structure one's life. Narrating is a common and crucial religious practice.

THE STORIES OF RELIGIOUS TRADITIONS

Religious traditions usually take a set of oral or written texts or narratives as in some way central. It has become a commonplace that religions are implicit or explicit narratives. Yet *how* religious traditions and narratives are connected is in dispute. For instance, religionists debate whether ritual or myth came first (temporally and logically) and theologians argue about the priority of narrative over doctrine. What is all too often forgotten is that there is no single type of religious narrative or storytelling practice any more than there is a single type of religious language or ritual. Within religious traditions, a wild variety of stories and purposes for storytelling abound.

For present purposes, I will classify stories functionally because how they function can shed some light on epistemic issues to be developed later.[7] First, one finds myths in religion. A myth is a story that establishes a world. A myth is neither true nor false in any simple or direct sense (but see Tilley 1985:182–213). Rather, it sets up the way a participant in the tradition learns how to dwell in the world as a whole. Often the basic religious myth is a story "out of time," set in a primordial or prehistoric or sacred time and in a place removed from the everyday. Generally speaking, myths narrate the beginning and end of the natural and social world and thus answer the great "why" questions. They usually function to direct religious awe, to provide a vision of order, and to establish the basic parameters of the society and one's place in it. In the sense used here, every tradition (including secular ones) carries or is constituted narratively by a myth. Learning how to understand the myth is learning to live in the world that the tradition creates.

Second, there are sagas. Sagas are stories of a people in the world, stories of how "our people" has developed. H. Richard Niebuhr (1944) identified these stories as "inner history." Sagas, like myths, provide order and establish parameters for social life; unlike myths, they cannot be stories set outside the world of time and space. If the opening chapters of Genesis are a myth, the narratives of the Exodus are a saga dear to the Abrahamic traditions. And beyond the saga of a people are sagas of families or extended families that tell of roots and shoots "in the old country" or of the trials and tribulations undergone during migration or because of slavery. Traditions may have many sagas; participants in the tradition learn to hear and tell these stories as a way of coming to understand their place in the universe. Obviously, both myths and sagas can marginalize some people or classes of people by placing them in demeaning positions; but in so doing, these stories become stimuli for the emergence of reformist or revolutionary practices or new traditions.

Third, most traditions carry trickster or parabolic stories. Literary critics, anthropologists, and psychologists have explored the trickster genre as stories of archetypal individuals who upset the expected norms and puncture pompous authorities, and parables as stories that upset myths. Many trickster or parabolic stories function as exemplary stories. But then these stories license ways of reforming, revising, and even rejecting the traditions. They provide often startling models for opening up the most closed systems.

Fourth, there are exemplary stories: stories of how to live and of what one ought to do in specific kinds of situations. There are stories that tell of Good Samaritans, parables of Gautama Buddha, and stories that tell how to get in position to realize the unity of Tao. These stories teach individuals both what is to be sought and how to seek. They may be true or false, oppressive or liberating, comforting or challenging, encouraging or threatening, etc. These stories provide the content of virtue and vice and the context for moral rules, which are often attributed to the gods or god or the nature of things. The best of them truly reveal what it is to live in and out of a tradition.

Prototypical narratives of literate traditions are often brought together in a normative collection such as the Hebrew and Christian Bibles. The endless debates over how a tradition forms a collection or how a text forms a tradition need not concern us here. They are clearly correlative in practice. What differs is the normative status of the texts.[8]

In the Christian traditions, there are numerous biographical and autobiographical conversion narratives. Many of them deal with the subject's response to God's touch on her or his soul. Only rarely do they deal with the circumstances in which the conversions occur. They often deal with God and the individual's soul, but ignore whatever mediates between God and them or provides the background for their "direct meetings" (if such occur). This focus is not surprising; after all, what matters to converts is not where they stood when God touched them, what color the walls were painted, or who influenced them, but the simple and obvious fact that it was *God* who changed their lives.

Such narratives provide models for the practice of a religious life. They can show how the tradition is incarnated in a specific human life. They can be exemplary stories, models for understanding what it means to become or to be a Christian. They also provide guidance to any who would want to share the tradition with others.

RELIGIOUS FOUNDERS AND EXEMPLARS

Participants in a religious tradition often are or try to be followers of a founder, model, or archetypal figure or of a path that such a figure created or discovered. Traditions can carry exemplary stories which hold up a person as an ideal to follow. One ought to follow the path of the Buddha; one ought to be like Jesus or the mother of Jesus; one ought to follow the Ten Commandments that God delivered through Moses. There may be religious traditions so austere that no individual or group may be exemplary in some sense, but I know of none.

An archetypal or stereotypical figure or a founder implicitly or explicitly sets a path that those who belong to the tradition try to follow. Christians will try to follow Jesus and the saints so that they get to heaven. Buddhists will try to walk the Eightfold Path so they will reach, be given, or achieve the cessation of suffering and craving that is Nirvana. Orthodox Jews will attempt to follow Torah, epitomized in the Law of Moses, as completely and as perfectly as possible, perhaps to hasten the day when the Messiah will rule. A proper Sunni Muslim will try to walk the straight path of a God-guided life, the *shari'ah*, and will be guided not only by the God-given *Qur'an*, but also by the *hadith*, the collection of reports of what Muhammad did and said. The paths religious folk walk vary with the traditions as well as the goals to which these paths lead.

One way in which religious "difficulty" surfaces is in the question over which path we ought walk and how we ought walk it. Often this is articulated as an academic issue. Is a life guided by the Ten Commandments or the Noble Eightfold Path a better life to live? Should one follow Moses or Jesus? For which, if any, should one decide?

But is this a matter of "decision"? *In vitro*, in the classroom, the implication is that one rationally chooses one's path. This is analogous to some epistemologists' presupposition that we choose (at least some of) our beliefs. *In vivo*, it is the rare belief over which we have direct or even indirect voluntary control. In most instances, we simply and properly form beliefs on the basis of what we're told, what we experience, or what we infer from other beliefs we hold—unless we have good reason in specific instances to doubt our authorities, our experience, or our inferences. Whatever decision may be involved in coming to believe, it is rarely, if ever, a completely unfettered decision to believe.

Imagine, for instance, that you are a confirmed atheist hiking through the desert wilderness with your friend Moshe. You notice a peculiar bush on fire nearby. It burns, but it is not burnt up. You both turn to look at the bush and hear a voice calling out, "Moshe, Moshe." Once your friend answers that he is there, the voice says, "Do not come near; take your shoes from your feet, for the place on which you stand is holy ground." What is it reasonable for you to believe? What is it reasonable for you to do?

You are skeptical. As an atheist with common sense, you look for a good reason for this apparently miraculous phenomenon. You check for a magician's trick. But you find no hidden speaker, no secret oil-fed torch in a fake bush, no good reason to doubt your eyes and ears. You splash water in your face to wake yourself up in case you're dreaming, you slap your temple in case you're hallucinating, you ask Moshe if he sees and hears what you do—only to discover his shoes are in his hands and his face is averted and he is shaking like a leaf. You don't want to believe this is happening; you want to believe that this theophany is a phony; you want to keep your shoes on and defy the trickster who is teasing you. But once you have checked as thoroughly as you can and found no good reason to doubt your senses or your inferences, can you will yourself into believing that nothing strange is going on? Can you will yourself to doubt? Is it wise for you to keep your shoes on or to kick them off as quickly as possible?

I would suggest that you really don't have full voluntary control over what you believe at this point. You have engaged your "overrider system," your usual strategy and tactics for weeding out unwarranted beliefs, and it has not given you sufficient reason to doubt your senses. You might "will" yourself not to believe, but the prudent action would be to remove your shoes—and to check later to find the deception, if you still thought you might have been deceived. And if you could find no deception later and did not try to deceive yourself into thinking it was a hallucination, you would be reasonable and prudent to recognize that such a theophany really occurred for you and that, at minimum, your valued atheism can no longer be your untroubled belief. You neither decided voluntarily to accept the evidence of your senses nor decided freely to doubt your faith. Rather, you were compelled to believe that you witnessed a theophany. Your belief was formed unavoidably when you could find no good reasons for doubting your initial impression. In fact, your doubt of atheism emerged against your will when your belief that the theophany occurred stood undefeated despite your best honest efforts to undermine it.

Having shared such an experience with Moshe, having heard him addressed by a Voice from the bush that you cannot reasonably doubt, and, having heard the Voice instruct Moshe to free God's people from bondage, is your choice to go with Moshe and to follow the path he will walk a matter of free choice? Obviously, you may not be the "slave-rescuing type," and so no experience could lead you on to such a path. But if you did not have a physical or psychological block against walking such a path, are you—not someone else, but you in your own situation as described—free simply to go on as before? While the answer to this moral question is not so obvious as the epistemic question noted above, your choice to walk on this path, to follow this man's way, is not a completely free choice. Later I will argue that the "will" does have a role to play in the proper formation of religious beliefs and the choice of religious paths and doxastic practices, but that role is indirect and neither necessary nor sufficient for a person to make a wise religious commitment.

The choice of religious exemplars to follow and religious paths to walk is not entirely up to us as individuals. It depends, in part, on the circumstances of our lives, on the options with which we are acquainted, on our luck or ability in being able to understand those practical options and their institutional and communal entanglements. But it also depends, in part, on our judgment about whether the path or paths that appeal to us lead us to a goal we wish to reach.

RELIGIOUS GOALS

Religious traditions hold out a final goal or ultimate blessing for the participants (and sometimes for all humanity). Some scholars find the prospect of reaching an ultimate goal the main reason people are religious. A "bottom-line-type" person might see the question about participation in a religious form of life as utilitarian: what do the adherents get out of participating? In popular discussions of religion, realizing such a goal, whether reaching the ultimate emptiness of Buddhist Nirvana or getting to the ultimate fullness of the Christian or Muslim heaven(s), is seen as a compelling motive and purpose for participating in a religious tradition. If you want to get to the other side of the lake, you take a boat that is heading in that direction.

However, the goal to be reached is not the whole story. Many religious traditions make a distinction that is especially important in Christianity and Pure Land Buddhism: the distinction between grace and works, or between getting what you deserve as a reward or punishment for your life or receiving as a gift that which fulfills one's ultimate desire or hope. The fact is that religious traditions have great difficulty expressing and figuring out how one reaches the goal of the path. Do the gods or God or the nature of things give it to you or do you earn it? Is the goal reached or realized (the verbs are neutral whether the goal is an "achievement" or a "gift") by individuals? by a remnant of humanity? by all humanity or by all living things? How inclusive is the goal?

Moreover, the very process of realizing the goals of religions is seen as worthwhile. As some Christians want to go to heaven or make heaven a reality on Earth, as most Communists want to bring about a classless society, as some Jews await the coming of the Messiah, as Buddhists seek to reach nirvana, so walking the path toward the future goal provides those on the path with present meaning in their lives. Religions not only provide an ultimate goal that is often beyond one's imagination, but also a proximate satisfaction in seeking that goal: meaningful life here and now despite death and destruction (see Berger 1967:81–101).

Religious traditions provide resolutions to the problems of suffering. These resolutions are not necessarily redemptive, that is, they do not always promise a new life after death or an absorption in the ocean of being. But they do provide life with meaning. Consider the great religious leader, Chairman Mao:

> All men must die, but death can vary in its significance. The ancient Chinese writer Szuma Chien said, 'Though death befalls all men alike, it may be heaver than Mt Tai or lighter than a feather.' To die for the people is of more weight than Mt Tai, but to work for the fascists and die for the exploiters and oppressors is lighter than a feather (quoted by Bowker 1970: 191).

A similar view is expressed by Dag Hammarskjöld in a series of *Markings* from 1957, when he was serving as Secretary General of the United Nations:

> Do not seek death. Death will find you. But seek the road which makes death a fulfillment.
>
> Your body must become familiar with its death—in all its possible forms and degrees—as a self-evident, imminent, and emotionally neutral step on the way towards the goal you have found worthy of your life.
>
> As an element in the sacrifice, death is a fulfillment, but more often it is a degradation, and never an elevation (Hammarskjöld 1964:136).

For both of these realistic people, the way one approaches death shapes the meaning of one's life. It is not merely the goal that makes the path worth walking, but the satisfactions received on the path that leads to the goal.

Religious traditions proffer different goals for human life. This diversity gives the traditions much of their attraction. They provide people with a meaningful life in the face of anomie, disaster, and death. Indeed, it is this trait that renders them liable to condemnation as "opiates." To neglect these goals and their differences when attempting to understand a religion or do philosophy of religion is to tell so truncated a version of their story that it is finally a falsification of what religion is and what participation in a religious tradition constitutes.

Neither practices nor narratives could exist, however, without being actually embodied in communities and institutions. Both are necessary parts of religion, without which a tradition could not exist. All too often theologians and philosophers overlook the importance of religious communities and institutions.

RELIGIOUS COMMUNITIES AND INSTITUTIONS

Traditions are passed on through local communities embedded in enduring institutions. This part of the picture is complex and controversial. The basic point is that a religious *tradition* cannot live without a *local community* and an *enduring institution*. Many religionists do not clearly distinguish the institutional from the communal and traditional elements of religion. Indeed, it is difficult to do so, for they are complexly intertwined.[9]

A rough and ready understanding of the differences of these elements can be seen by describing the way they divide. *Communities* split or separate or send out colonies; fissures in *institutions* are schisms; defalcations from *traditions* are heresies. Often heresy and schism are linked (many, but not all, apostates are both heretics and schismatics), but they are not identical. And communities often split (e.g., conventual motherhouses establish daughterhouses, elder churches spin off daughter churches) even though there is no heresy or schism. The importance of making such distinctions suggests that the communal, institutional, and traditional elements of religion can and must be distinguished, even if they cannot be separated. If philosophers are to do philosophy of religion, they cannot ignore these realities.

First, by "institution" I mark the structures that Max Weber (1947) described as developing when charismatic authority is routinized. Although Weber was concerned with detailing patterns of authority, his work also shows how we can distinguish the institutional element proper from the communal and traditional elements in religion.

Weber claims that a community can be formed around the authority of a charismatic figure and may exist without any formal institutional structures—for a time. But such communities cannot endure beyond the leader's death or loss of charisma unless that charisma is routinized into an organizational structure that gives persons official authority. Weber (1947) put it this way:

> In its pure form charismatic authority has a character specifically foreign to every-day routine structures. The social relationships directly involved are strictly personal, based on this validity and practice of charismatic personal qualities. If this is not to remain a purely transitory phenomenon, but to take on the character of a permanent relationship forming a stable community of disciples or band of followers or a party organization or any sort of political or hierocratic organization, it is necessary for the character of charismatic authority to become radically changed. Indeed, in its pure form charismatic authority may be said to exist only in the process of originating. It cannot remain stable but becomes either traditionalized or rationalized, or a combination of both (363–64).

Weber delineates two types of institutional religious authority. Institutional authority based on "legal patterns of normative rules and the right of those elevated to authority under such rules to issue commands" is *rational* authority; institutional authority "resting on an established belief in the sanctity of immemorial traditions and the legitimacy of the status of those exercising authority under them" is *traditional* authority (Weber 1947:328). Both sorts of authority create offices, one of whose main purposes is to replicate a pattern of practices and beliefs inaugurated by the charismatic figure, that is, forming a tradition.

Great religious figures draw disciples into a community; but when the figure is gone, the only way for the community to endure is routinization of charisma. The structures that emerge to "carry on" and "develop" the traditions inaugurated by the founder are religious institutions. These institutions make possible a transmission of tradition to second- and third-generation disciples of the leader, whether those disciples are distant from the leader in time (as Weber seems to assume) or in location (a point Weber seems to ignore, for first-generation disciples may be given authority to speak in the leader's name beyond the immediate locale of the leader). Leaders who may not have the charismatic authority of the founder acquire authority because they take on an official role. They may be named to office by the leader or placed in office by other means in the leader's absence. The origins and development of institutional authority and authorities in Christianity, in the various Islamic traditions, in the Jesuits or any other religious order with a charismatic founder, and even in enduring institutions such as the National Baptist Convention, are merely a few of the historical examples that illustrate Weber's "charisma and routinization" thesis.

Although contemporary critical theorists have propounded more nuanced theories of society than Weber's, his basic distinction between "charismatic" and "institutional" authority is quite adequate for present purposes, if it is read "dialectically" rather than "monodirectionally," and if it is not associated with negative value claims about the irrationality of religion that seem typical of Weber.

The gifts of charismatic figures are constituted, in part, by institutional authorities, communal relationships, and the beliefs and practices of traditions. Their contributions are never, and could never be, purely original, as a "monodirectional" reading of the relationship between charismatic and institutional authority would suggest. Charismatic authority emerges in social contexts that are *given*. Such inherited traditions are the lodes from which meanings are *taken*. The power of charismatic persons comes, in part, from their ability to reshape the given by taking meaning from it in new, unconventional ways, to communicate that meaning to others, and thus to inspire a new community with a nascent tradition. Traditions are not essentially deformative nor institutions essentially alienating as a monodirectional analysis (whether classic Marxian, Weberian, or other) might suggest. Von Hügel's more dialectical reading of these relationships (1904) provides a useful corrective to Weber.

Institutions are not "systems" which "colonize the lifeworld," to use Habermas's terms, for these "systems" are modern instantiations of power and economy dissociated from the lifeworld—from the spaces in which we live most of the time and which provide most of the meaning of our lives. "Institutions," as used here, are constituents necessary for a lifeworld to exist and endure—as Habermas himself notes (1983:12–14). Weber's analysis, unlike Habermas's, does not presume the modern split between system and lifeworld, and is thus applicable beyond modernity.

Indeed, one cannot seek the bearer of absent charismatic authority except through what the institutional authorities have preserved and replicated as the tradition. The quests for such fascinating historical figures as Kung Fu Tzu, Jesus, or Muhammed are possible only because their charismatic powers have been routinized and preserved in practices and texts in an enduring institution. It may be obvious, but it is often ignored: institutions are not necessarily "deteriorations" of charismatic authority or real religion, but transformations of authority without which there is *no practically possible retrieval* of that authority and *no practically possible access* to that charismatic figure, and *no practically possible continuity of* his or her distinctive gifts and insights, once the charismatic figure and immediate memory of her or him is gone.

It is a commonplace that institutional patterns of authority and power are enormously varied and complex. In the Christian traditions, institutional authorities have usually been clerics. In Islam, for instance, the *imam* is properly not a cleric, but a lay prayer leader; although he has authority for the local community gathered in the mosque, he may or may not have institutional authority beyond the local community. In both traditions, political rulers often have tremendous institutional authority, as demonstrated, for example, when the Emperor Constantine convoked and set the agenda for the Council of Nicea in 326 C.E. The "lay follower"/"cleric leader" pattern typical of Christianity is one of many institutional patterns, all of which function more or less well to empower officeholders to guide the community as it carries on and passes on a tradition.

One important implication of Weber's thesis is that there can be a religious community (such as one gathered around a charismatic figure) that is not a religious institution. The leader's charismatic presence can make official authority superfluous. But that community is inevitably locatable only in one place (unless the charismatic figure can bilocate) and dies if it does not become institutionalized. For present purposes, it is sufficient to note that enduring religions have both institutional and communal elements. But the key point is that this distinction is not merely nominal: communities can exist without institutional authorities.

A significant characteristic of a community formed around a charismatic leader is that it is *gathered*. This factor marks the communal, as opposed to the institutional, aspect of enduring religions. The Catholic Church as an institution is worldwide; the Catholic Church as a parish or base community or religious house is gathered and local. Some theologians have marked this distinction with the *ecclesiolae in ecclesia* formula. But the institutional/communal distinction is not the same as one between the local and the universal or translocal church. A Baptist church with a thoroughly congregational polity may be necessarily local, but that does not mean it is not both a community and an institution. The "First Baptist" churches in many towns or cities of the American South have become enduring bureaucratic, even hierarchical, institutions that are part of the power structure of their hometowns. Having a deeply communitarian ideology and local autonomy does not preclude a church from simultaneously being a hierocratic institution. Indeed, if such a church is to endure and gather new generations of worshipers, it must have an institutional structure.

Second, by "communities" I mean to mark that "gathered" aspect of a religion. Edward Farley (1990) has helpfully used E. Levinas's notion of the "community of the face" to define "community" in this sense as "a social group in which face-to-face relations are valued and pursued for their own sake. Face-to-face relations are part of the raison d'etre of a village, therapy group, and some kinds of schools. Accordingly, in most instances, a small village is a community and a staff of researchers is not" (Farley, 290). For Farley, Christian and Jewish communities have been prime examples of such face-to-face

communities. In writing of communities, as distinguished from institutions, I mean to highlight these gatherings in which "face-to-face
relations" are central and distinctive.[10]

Generally speaking, a person is raised in a religious tradition and
is initiated into religious life in a local community. In most societies,
communal leaders and familial authorities teach a person; their authority is traditional in Weber's sense. One's father, one's mother, one's
aunts, one's uncles, the local shaman, the monk, the missionary, the
rabbi, the minister, the Director of Religious Education, or some other
familial or communal authority initiate a person into religious practice
and belief. Although these authorities may be officially designated,
the tradition is learned face-to-face.

People who convert to a religion generally learn the tradition in
a community. They may be converted by people whose authority
is more rational or traditional than charismatic. Conversion is not
necessarily induced by a charismatic figure. Missionaries even learn
recipes for reaching potential converts and revivals become routinized.
And in the United States at least, most conversions are effected by
personal contact with a small group, with and in a local, even familial,
community.[11]

When learners are tested to see if they have understood the
tradition, the testing is done by designated authorities who function
as institutional authorities charged with preserving and extending the
tradition. One person may assume both roles of teacher and tester. But
the teacher primarily functions face-to-face, while the tester primarily
functions as an officer empowered to decide if the learner has understood the tradition sufficiently to be a full member. Whether one is
born into a religion or converted into a religion, generally speaking,
a gathered community shapes one's religious life and one's entry into
the religion.

Leaders of a local community may have their *formal* authority
from their office (institutional authority). However, their *effective* authority for initiating others into the tradition requires a face-to-face
relationship. Obviously, these relationships, although interpersonal,
are not necessarily friendships between equals. Various modes of
relationship may be appropriate depending on the circumstances.

As local, then, a religious community gathers face to face, and
is constituted by interpersonal and social relationships. This definition
does not, however, preclude translocal gatherings, such as revivals,
missions, camp meetings, or other larger assemblies. Given modern

telecommunications, a community may not even be located in the same place, but may nonetheless be "gathered," at least in an extended sense. Thus, being localized may be a common sign of, but not a necessary characteristic of, a gathered community.

That an individual ordinarily learns how to participate in a tradition through participation in face-to-face relationships does not deny the importance of official authority in a local community.[12] Communities can certainly exhibit and even be constituted by routinized authority. However, especially in a pluralistic society where members may find that leaving a community is a "live option," local, gathered communities flourish where face-to-face relationships are valued and strong. It is these relationships that make official authority *effective* in a gathered community in a pluralistic social context.

The communal element, then, must be distinguished from the institutional element of religion. Face-to-face religious communities form themselves when and where folk join in the practices of realizing (making real) a religious tradition. These places may be called churches, mosques, synagogues, monasteries, or ashrams, etc. A gathered community may constitute itself for a brief time and then evaporate, as happens in some revivals in the United States when charismatic authority is not routinized. People with official status may participate in and may well have authority in local communities, but that does not mean that local communities are necessarily institutions.

This difference between the institutional and the communal elements of religion is not merely nominal. The reality of the distinction is noted in the fact that not all members of a religion can perform some speech acts recognized in that tradition while all members can perform some other speech acts. That is, some speech acts are "institutionally bound" and some are "institutionally free." A speech act is institutionally free if the conditions for performing it do not require that the speaker have a specific role or status in the institution. A speech act is institutionally bound if the conditions for performing it do require that the speaker have a specific role or status in the institution. For instance, engaging in petitionary prayer or saying a creed does not require that the person so acting have a specific role or status in any religious institution. Any member of the community, even an alienated one, can perform these speech acts once they have learned the practice; and it would be odd (but not impossible) for someone outside this community that believes in prayer and takes a specific creed as normative to pray for help or recite the creed.

On the other hand, in contemporary Roman Catholicism, for example, only the pope has the institutional position and authority to *declare* a dogma divinely revealed, for example, "that the Immaculate Mother of God, the ever Virgin Mary, having completed the course of her earthly life, was assumed body and soul into heavenly glory" (DS 3903). Yet any member of the Christian community believing the doctrine can *profess* this dogma in appropriate circumstances. Similarly, any Catholic may *say* or *pray* the words of the eucharistic consecration as a member of the worshiping community, but only a properly ordained priest can *in saying them* consecrate the elements (see Tilley 1991:33–34). Different members of the same community may have different institutional status and may be enabled to, or disabled from, performing certain speech acts. Speech act analysis reinforces the significance of the distinction between institutional and communal elements of religion. The distinction is real even though in actual practice these elements are rarely separated.

Third, both institutions and communities must be distinguished from "traditions." Institutions carry traditions, but these are not convertible terms. Learning a tradition cannot be reduced to participation in a community or accepting an institutional authority structure. One may know the Baptist tradition, for instance, but not be a participant in it.

How institutions are constituted affects the viability of the tradition they carry. The most obvious example of institutional corruption undermining effective communication of a religious tradition is the late medieval church. The need for institutional reform was obvious, and reforms were attempted before the Reformation. However, definitive reform only occurred after the institutional schism of the Reformation. One may also think of the collapse of some of the televangelistic ministries in this country. Corruption in institutions or of institutional officers can destroy a community and undermine a tradition.

An institutional authority cannot guarantee that its pronouncements will become part of the lived tradition that sustains the community. Perhaps the most obvious example here is the refusal of Roman Catholic communities to accept the institutional authorities' finding that "artificial" contraception is intrinsically evil. Although it is a practice forbidden by the institutional authorities, many members of the community engage in it without serious qualms. In the American branch of the Roman Catholic Church, laity are far more willing to have married men and women ordained priests than are the official authorities. At present, the institutionally imposed discipline is accepted by those who remain in the church, but as the number of celibate male clergy diminish, the discipline may be abrogated (as it already has been in the case of converting, conservative Protestant clergy) or Roman Catholics may abandon the church. In short, institutional authority is not always effective in and accepted by the community: communities may be creative in transforming the tradition they embody and pass on; other traditions may be lost or transformed regardless of what official authorities mandate.

The point of this chapter so far has been to consider religion as "a set of powerful *practices* that embody the life-forming convictions of its practitioners" (McClendon), to sketch out some patterns those practices typically take, and to argue that these patterns are distinguishable from, but not separable from, the communities that communicate them and the institutions that carry them. We turn now to work in the philosophy of religion. But if this chapter is anywhere close to correct in its understanding of how the elements of religion hang together, then most philosophy of *religion* is rational *theology* in disguise.

RELIGION AND EPISTEMOLOGY

As we saw in the previous chapter, modern religious epistemologists have generally followed the individualistic and wholly theoretical approach characteristic of modern epistemology and modern philosophy of religion. Modern philosophical critics of religion (such as Hume and Russell) and philosophical friends of religion (such as James and Plantinga) have focused on individuals' religious beliefs (and, occasionally, their practices). The key question for the modern epistemologist is whether an individual is entitled to believe a proposition p, or is justified in believing p, or holds p on the basis of a reliable belief-forming mechanism operating in a proper environment, etc. Rarely have the social processes and methods of belief formation been examined. Even those general epistemologists who find social constituents of knowing important (e.g., Goldman) defer examining them until the issues of individual cognition are worked out. As Code (1991) points out, "an obsession with the autonomy of reason that manifests itself in a conception of knowers as isolated and essentially self-sufficient beings, who are self-reliant in knowledge seeking, has characterized mainstream epistemology" (268). The individualistic presumptions characteristic of much religious epistemology simply parallel the paradigms of epistemology and modern philosophy of religion. Yet this individualistic approach is at least in tension with the understanding of religion prevalent in the academy and summarized in the descriptive definition that I have explored in this chapter.[13]

In general, I find no good argument for taking an individual's bare entitlement to believe a proposition *p* as showing one reasonable or wise in accepting *p* as a basic or central and distinctive religious belief or in participating in a religious tradition. Examining an individual's entitlement to *p* as a proposition focuses on a threefold abstraction from its normal context. First, it abstracts *p* from a web or pyramid of beliefs the individual holds. Second, it ignores the important case noted by Pascal, Newman, and others, of the real differences between the person who gives nominal belief in a proposition and the one who gives real assent to a religion and the ways of life it promotes. Third, it separates the individual from the practices, communities, and institutions in which that belief is formed. Since the way a belief fits into a belief system (and into a life) determines, at least in part, its meaning, it is not clear how such *in vitro* examination of a specific individual or proposition tells us about beliefs *in vivo*. The other beliefs that an individual holds, one's attitudes, and the religious practices in which he or she participates are all derived in some way from the community and institution in which the individual participates and its practices and traditions. To abstract a single proposition from a belief system is a practice that makes it easy to ignore how that belief fits into an individual's life and the actual meaning it has there.

Of course, a philosopher may want to defend the possibility that a religious believer is entitled to hold a proposition such as "God speaks to me through this book," or "God appears to me in my experience." But the context for such an argument is polemical. The philosopher is *defending* a belief, person, or practice against the attacks of an adversary. As in military battles, so in such academic skirmishes: the direction of the attacks is likely to determine the shape of the defense.

Cultured despisers of religion from David Hume to J. L. Mackie and beyond set the place and style of battle by the way they attack the reasonableness of theological propositions. Other philosophers respond to these attacks, and if their responses are to be relevant, they must focus on the charges the opponents make. Because the challenge is often to the rationality of holding a religious belief, for example, the belief that God exists, the religious epistemologist's primary purpose is often merely to defend an individual's entitlement to hold that proposition.

Yet neither attack nor defense are appropriate if one's object is to understand how people come to undertake religious practices, to know religious concepts, and to evaluate religious commitments. We no longer need assume that the philosophy of religion should only examine and analyze isolated theological concepts or propositions individuals hold (which is what modern antagonists attack). Nor should we presume that these propositions are sufficient to constitute religious belief or to stand in for a religious tradition in the philosophy of religion. Philosophy of religion, as opposed to philosophical defense or rational theology, requires a comprehensive understanding of religion.[14] An epistemology conceived of as a practical account of the wisdom of religious commitment needs to focus on religion qua religion, or even on a specific religion, not on individual propositions or theological concepts abstracted from life.

In the next chapter, we will examine two patterns in philosophy of religion. The first pattern takes religious propositions as able to "stand in for" religion in the attempt to validate religious belief. It follows a now-classic path in modern philosophy of religion. Although it will ultimately be found wanting, even on its own terms, we can learn from it. The second pattern is a practical approach. It is a marked improvement over the modern rationalist approaches, yet this pattern, too, is helpful but incomplete; it ignores the connections between the elements of religion.

NOTES TO CHAPTER 2

1. Gallagher (1993) argues that the classic account of Nock (1933) relies excessively on William James for his account of conversion and too little on the literature he considered, resulting in an unwarranted individualism and neglect of the community's importance for conversion in his account. Lash (1988) makes a similar point about James's individualism.

2. McClendon differs from MacIntyre (1981) in allowing that the *teloi* of practices are not necessarily internal to those practices and in claiming that practices, even if one engages in them properly, do not necessarily require morally good means, develop virtuous practitioners, or lead to good ends.

3. Notice that I am not saying that one has to accept or believe in the doctrine to understand it, but that one must understand practically (*"in vivo*, not *in vitro"*) how the doctrine fits within the discourse system. All I am claiming is that a position of "descriptive reductionism" is untenable (see Proudfoot 1985).

4. Conversely, one can engage in petitionary prayer even if one does not believe that God exists (Tilley 1991:56–63). Thus, religious practice, normally a constituent of person's religious commitment along with specific beliefs and attitudes, is not necessarily connected with a propositional belief in God's existence, although it is ordinarily so connected.

5. D. Z. Phillips has made similar points in his numerous writings. I, however, recognize that it may be *possible* in specific contexts and for specific purposes to abstract propositions from their religious context. Because I find practices related not only to communities, but also to institutions, I see that in a context of religious diversity, it may be possible wisely to choose one religious commitment over another.

6. One neglected exception is Ian Ramsey's work on "cosmic disclosures" which give rise to "discernment and commitment" and which are both generated by, and evocative of, "qualified models" of God (Ramsey 1957: 173–79); Christians are, according to Ramsey, to read "God" as "Trinity" (although Muslims and Jews must not).

7. The rest of this section reflects and elaborates ideas first developed in Tilley (1985), chapters 1 and 3.

8. This difference is especially clear when one considers the varied practices of interpreting the Christian Bible. Some, often identified as "fundamentalists," take the very words of the text as words dictated by God, and thus infallible, inspired, inerrant, perfect. The normativity of the texts is understood in a very literalistic, straightforward way. Other groups recognize the compositeness of the Christian Bible and the difficulties of taking a text with internal difficulties or contradictions as literally normative. Many of these groups look for a single criterion within the text as a key to their understanding. They may take the New Testament as key to the Hebrew Bible, or the writings of Paul as key for the whole, or the teaching of Jesus as the norm by which all other writings are to be interpreted. Others recognize the compositeness of the texts and the multiple authors of the books that compose it. They recognize that the actual text is variant in many places and that the limits of the canon are disputed. Thus, they will see the text as a portrayal of prototypical, not archetypical, Christianity. For each of these groups, the biblical text is normative, but it is normative in very different ways.

9. See Tilley (1994) for an extended version of this argument, including an analysis of how the institutional and communal elements of religion are necessary for individuals to have religious experiences, even "breathtakingly novel" ones.

10. In any institution, interpersonal relations may also be important. In institutional contexts, however, such relationships may be cultivated as the *means* to ensure institutional or professional goals; in face-to-face communities, these relationships are *ends* sought for their own sake.

11. See, for instance, Stark and Bainbridge (1985). As their research shows, "Social networks play an essential role in recruitment to cults, sects, and conventional denominations" (322).

12. Jürgen Habermas (1987) recognizes this point when he claims, "Communicative actions are . . . processes of social integration and socialization" (139). At this point Habermas is distancing himself from P. Berger and T. Luckman, who construe "cultural reproduction" as mere "reduplication" of the "lifeworld," according to Habermas. The transmission of tradition is not merely reproductive, but also creative, a point obscured by Burger and Luckman (as influenced by Weber). Habermas goes on to note, "While participants in interaction, turned 'toward the world,' reproduce, through their accomplishments of mutual understanding, the cultural knowledge on which they draw, they simultaneously reproduce their memberships in collectivities and their identities. When one of these other aspects shifts into the foreground, the concept of the lifeworld is again given a one-sided formulation: it is narrowed down either in an *institutionalistic* or in a *sociopsychological* fashion" (ibid). Recognizing both institutional and communal elements in religion avoids the imbalance: the institution preserves and transmits the tradition, the face-to-face community socializes individuals into it—and develops the tradition in the process of inculturation into new contexts.

13. Such tension in itself does not mean that only one approach is right. Indeed, some philosophers and some social scientists may be seeking answers to such diverse questions that their investigative and analytical practices may be so different as to be incommensurable. Nonetheless, if one is to do philosophy of *religion*, and if religious belief cannot stand in for religion as a whole, then one needs at least a working definition of what religion is.

14. I do not mean to deny that philosophers of religion do splendid work on the analysis of religious doctrines or that such work should not contribute to theology and catechetics (see D'Arcy 1991). But philosophy of religion cannot be limited to such work.

3

Justifying Religious Belief in Modern Religious Epistemology

Many modern philosophers of religion seem to presume that if they can show that a religious believer is justified or warranted in holding a belief which is central to a religious tradition, they have shown that the believer's commitment to that tradition is reasonable. Their presumption is called the "presumption of substitutability" because, for them, resolving the questions of the rationality of religious beliefs stands in for resolving the question of whether a person ought to be religious. If they don't have or make that presumption or something like it, then either they are not interested in religion as practiced, in which case the arguments are relevant only to disembodied academic minds; or they must presume that being religious is essentially believing certain propositions, a position that the previous chapter has shown won't do. This chapter examines three exemplary attempts to justify religious belief by Christian philosophers.

Some philosophical theologians, exemplified here by Richard Swinburne, approach this task by seeking to show the rational probability of ultimate beliefs, that is, those beliefs having to do with ultimate reality (whether God, the world, the mind or something else) that are central strands in a web of belief. Beyond the problems with this approach noted in chapter 2, those who use it to defend the rationality of theism often run into the "problem of parity." Although I will argue that Swinburne's position is finally unsatisfactory, his "progressive" notion of rationality is of great use for understanding the wisdom of religious commitment.

In publishing a long-awaited philosophical tour de force, Alvin Plantinga has claimed that traditional theists are in a better epistemic position than materialists. He has constructed a version of a "naturalistic approach to epistemology." Naturalized epistemologies claim that how our belief-acquiring processes actually work is strongly relevant to questions about whether we have properly arrived at our beliefs. "Descriptive questions about belief acquisition have an important bearing on normative questions about belief acquisition" (Kornblith 1985:3). Plantinga reaches the startling conclusion that it is more rational for naturalist epistemologists to be metaphysical supernaturalists than to be metaphysical naturalists. Or to put it more crudely, that without accepting a belief that there is a God, the best contemporary epistemologies have a conceptual hole in their middle. I will argue that however important Plantinga's arguments are for developing a rational theology, they do not help resolve the problem of "many practices."[1]

William P. Alston remains within the now dominant strand of "naturalized epistemology," but moves away from Swinburne's rationalism and Plantinga's epistemological basis for rational theology. He concentrates on showing that participating in religious practices provides a way of formulating a theory of the reasonableness of holding religious beliefs. Alston's contribution marks a major turn to a practical epistemology and to focusing on religious practice and belief, rather than on rational theology. Although it neglects the institutional element of religion, Alston's focus on practices provides a more substantial epistemology of religious belief and provides a bridge from the rationalists' attempts to warrant or justify religious belief to our argument for seeking the wisdom of religious commitment—to which we will turn in the next chapter.

THE PARITY PROBLEM AND
THE PROBABILITY OF THEISM

The great problem facing modern philosophical arguments to show religious belief justified on rational grounds is the problem of parity. The historic 1948 BBC debate between Frederick Copleston, S.J., and Bertrand Russell (Hick 1964:167–94) provides a classic example of the problem. Both participants constructed arguments in support of the reasonableness of their key claims. Yet neither could show his position more reasonable than the other or demonstrate that the other's position was unreasonable. Perhaps the best verdict on the debate is a "Scotch verdict": both sides have "not proven" their claims, and neither side has defeated the other's claims. The result of the argument leaves the two sides on a par with each other.

Intuitively, one suspects that numerous ultimate beliefs are on roughly the same epistemic footing. Christian beliefs about God, Theravadin claims about Nirvana and dependent co-origination, and secular humanists' agnosticism about the ultimate may all be roughly in the same epistemic realm: not proven, not defeated. As these beliefs, not to mention others, can be shown to be coherent, to fit fairly well with what we know of the world, and to have some external support, they appear to be on a par with each other. On the "presumption of substitutability," showing that a believer is entitled to his ultimate beliefs demonstrates the rationality of adopting or holding the set of beliefs for which those ultimate beliefs are central. But if that is true, then all of these beliefs seem rational and, given the presumption, the religious traditions themselves are apparently on an epistemic par.

Such a state of affairs supports a form of religious indifference: if a number of belief systems are equally reasonable to hold or adopt, then it is (at least epistemically) indifferent which system, if any, one holds.[2] Epistemic parity combined with the presumption of substitutability either yields religious indifferentism (it doesn't matter if one participates in one religion or another) or implies religious commitment to be irrational or nonrational (the choice between beliefs is at best a matter of taste or training, and at worst a matter of luck or whim). Such an intellectually indifferent result, however, lands some religious thinkers in a dilemma.

If, on the one hand, one set of beliefs about the ultimate is more rationally supportable than the others, then the apparent inability of demonstrating its rationality is embarrassing, to say the least. Such failure casts doubt about the use of rational procedures for deciding religious belief. If investigation, argument, or evidence cannot show one set of ultimate beliefs certain or more probable than its competitors, and if a rational person believes a proposition only if it is at least more probably true than its competitors, then rational procedures are not the necessary or sufficient way to find reasonable ultimate beliefs. If, on the other hand, all ultimate beliefs are on a par with each other, then rational procedures may not be undermined. However, such marshalling of evidence, reminders, and arguments only shows that accepting one ultimate belief is no more rational than accepting another. One is perhaps rational in accepting any one of them, even if they contradict each other. Or perhaps it is rational to suspend belief in the face of such parity of support. This *prima facie* inability to decide among such candidates for beliefs on the basis of investigation, evidence, and argument, as demonstrated in the Russell-Copleston debates and many others, constitutes the problem of parity.

There are, however, different forms of "parity arguments" and different forms of the "problem of parity." To be fair to philosophers who make the "presumption of substitutability," we need to be clear about the differences.

In response to challenges which claim that Christian faith is incoherent, some philosophers have constructed defenses to show that a set of propositions central to traditional forms of Christian faith is not self-contradictory, for example, the free will defense as a response to the logical problem of evil (cf. Tilley 1984; and 1991:130–33). Others have explored various Christian doctrines to discover whether they are coherent and compatible with other things a Christian traditionally believes (cf. Swinburne 1977; Morris 1986a). Both types of argument share a characteristic: they assume Christian faith as a given and then seek to show that holding Christian theism, as a set of propositions expressing the central convictions of that faith, is not unreasonable.

Some critics have taken such arguments as though they were intended to warrant the propositions or set of propositions discussed, rather than to explore their senses or defend their compatibility.[3] Such critics evidently assimilate these arguments to what Terence Penelhum (1983) has called classical versions of the Parity Argument, which he identifies as *negative* parity arguments:

> The classical versions of the [Parity] Argument . . . suggest that the unbeliever, since he depends in his daily life upon commitments he does not, and cannot, found on reason and evidence, is in fact acting inconsistently when he refuses to embrace religious faith also, particularly if the reason he gives for his refusal is the fact that it cannot be founded in such a manner (150).

Negative parity arguments attempt to show that skeptics are inconsistent in their own beliefs while believers are not, so that religious believers are more rational than skeptics. Thus, the believer seeks to show that faith and skepticism are not on an epistemic par with each other by showing that the skeptic's position is inferior to the believer's. However, as Penelhum (1983:140–44) points out, arguments like David Hume's, which show that a metaphysical skepticism is as consistent with the practices of our common life as metaphysical theism, can provide resources sufficient to construct a refutation of this sort of negative parity argument.[4]

In contrast, *permissive* parity arguments, those characteristic of Norman Malcolm (1977) and the earlier work of Alvin Plantinga (1981: 1983), only attempt to show that religious belief is not irrational; they do not try to prove that skepticism is irrational. These arguments claim that all people are necessarily committed to ultimate principles that argument cannot justify. If each has differing properly basic beliefs[5] or a consistent set of framework principles, a believer cannot show a nonbeliever irrational in rejecting religious belief, and a nonbeliever cannot show a believer irrational in accepting belief in God. Both are on an epistemic par with each other, and both sets of beliefs are rationally *permissible* (given a minimum standard of rationality as a coherent set of framework principles or basic beliefs). Penelhum's distinguishing two forms of "parity argument" helpfully reveals the real force of some recent arguments in which believers attempt to provide a rational foundation for religious belief. In effect, this position accepts the stalemate between believer and skeptic (Copleston and Russell's debate for instance) and admits that both are within their epistemic rights to believe what they do and to resist the arguments of the other.

The utility of Penelhum's analysis of the different parity arguments can be shown by extending it to the arguments of some of the cultured despisers of religion. For instance, Antony Flew seeks to show religious belief incoherent, in effect constructing another sort of *negative* parity argument, by showing that religious belief is not on an epistemic par with atheism. But to justify his standards, he makes a circular argument. In *God and Philosophy* (1966), for instance, Flew writes:

> We therefore conclude, though as always subject to correction by further evidence and further argument, that the universe itself is ultimate; and hence, that whatever science may from time to time hold to be the most fundamental laws of nature must, *equally provisionally*, be taken as the last words in any series of answers to questions as to why things are as they are. The principles of the world lie themselves "inside" the world (194).[6]

But Flew's concept of evidence limits evidence to scientific evidence. No evidence other than evidence gathered presuming the validity of scientific approaches is permitted. For instance, Flew construes religious experience impermissible as evidence because it is "impossible to rely for proof upon some supposedly self-authenticating experience" (1966:132), that is, it fails to meet scientific standards because it is not publicly observable or repeatable.

In a more recent essay, he spells out this rejection of the evidential validity of religious experience:

> For they all know, just as well as everyone else knows, that, whenever and wherever they themselves claim to be enjoying their brand of supposedly cognitive religious experience, there is nothing available to be perceived, other than what is perceptible equally by all the rest of us; and, hence, that they are to all appearance engaged in nothing more or other than exercises of the imagination (Flew 1985:107).

No evidence is permitted that would count against the principles by which evidence is gathered. Flew's framework principles give meaning to his concept of evidence, so he cannot use what the principles construe as evidence to justify the principles without circular argument. And those principles exclude evidence that religious believers may find cogent.

Further, there is no reason to think that the universal availability of an experience is, as Flew presumes, a *proper* criterion for evidential reliability: after all John H. Watson could see what Sherlock Holmes could see ("perceptible by all"), but Holmes could also *see* much more than Watson (see Alston 1991). Thus, Flew's attempt to construct a *negative* parity argument, which would show the believer in a weaker epistemic position than the nonbeliever, fails in the same way that theologians' attempts to construct negative parity arguments generally fail.

In contrast, some philosophers have attempted to construct *permissive* parity arguments to show that a person can affirm the meaningfulness of life and the viability of morality without accepting a religious foundation for those affirmations. Some of Kai Nielsen's many arguments against belief in God fit this category. He has argued that one can affirm the meaningfulness of human life without reference to God or any transcendent meaning (1985).[7]

Nielsen's argument has two parts. His preliminary argument seeks to show that no good reason exists to believe in God or a supreme Good. His strategy is to show that direct arguments in support of the existence of God do not entail their conclusions, and that fideistic rejections of foundational arguments "scandalize" the intellect (1985:92). He rejects the cogency of both internalist and externalist approaches to supporting religious belief. Of course, that arguments do not entail their conclusions does not render those conclusions incredible, but merely unsupported by those arguments. And the scandalized intellect is Nielsen's own. A religious believer may feel no need to reduce or counter his scandal, especially if the believer has belief in God among her or his basic beliefs. Nor is it clear how Nielsen can show that his being scandalized is more rational than the believers' believing in God. Although Nielsen finds fideists irrational, his argument shows only that they have not proven their position. Nielsen has not succeeded in constructing a negative parity argument. His arguments do, however, support the first part of a permissive parity argument.

The second part of Nielsen's argument is his showing that even if there is no reason to believe in God or a Supreme Good, "there is no reason to conclude from this that morality crumbles or that life is meaningless" (1985:97). The strategy of the argument is to show that morality is independent of divine command and to discriminate the various meanings of "meaning" to show that a person's belief that life can be meaningful does not entail belief that the universe is meaningful. The statement of his claim concludes with a frankly personal rejection of religious claims:

> The wish to live forever for many of us is idle, something we are concerned neither to accept nor to reject. It is not true that if we no longer entertain these wishes our lives will become meaningless, fragmented, emotionally crippled; it is not true that given our atheistic intellectual convictions, our lives are something to be stoically endured with nihilism at the door. Fideists should not flatter themselves with the conceit that their response is the deepest, most human response to nonevasive reflection about our condition (101).[8]

Nielsen shows that it is not incoherent to believe that life can be meaningful without reference to God or another transcendent standard. And since atheism is at least *prima facie* coherent, it is rationally permissible to hold it until it is defeated.

If Nielsen's arguments are sustained, the result is a stalemate. Finally, neither the cultured despiser nor the believer can *prove* the other incoherent or in an inferior epistemic position. The believer can show the permissibility of her or his view of the ground of morality and the meaning of life, but not the impermissibility of the atheists' views. The despiser can show the permissibility of the atheistic view of the ground of morality and the meaning of life, but not the impermissibility of the believer's convictions.[9] These views are on an epistemic par.

Given such epistemic parity, Penelum's conclusion, that "our world is *intellectually ambiguous*" (1983:156), acquires even more significance. The agnostic or atheist apparently cannot be shown irrational in refusing to believe in God and the believer cannot be shown irrational in accepting such belief. Atheism is as defensible as theism, for atheists like Nielsen can defend their system of belief from external attack as well as believers can. Moreover, any system of thought with a framework that is not demonstrably self-contradictory and can account reasonably well for "common sense facts" about the world seems at least minimally defensible. But this parity presents a "significant theological *problem*. For what reason could there be for unbelievers always to have reasonable grounds for their hesitations?" (1983:158). While such a question may not be unanswerable, it requires an explanation, which for a Christian, must be consistent with what else a Christian believes. And this requirement is, as Penelhum points out, a serious theological problem, although he offers no solution for it.[10]

Richard Swinburne has deployed an argument which, if successful, would show that these ultimate beliefs are not on an epistemic par with each other. He has mounted a head-on attack on the "problem of parity," by attempting to construct a modern, probabilistic negative parity argument. His point is to show that theism is superior to atheism by being more probable than atheism. However, his view, while very instructive for understanding that "rationality" is not a univocal term, finally fails to show theism more rational than its competitors.

If a theologian or rational believer could show that a Christian belief system is more probable than an opposing system of belief, then (remembering the "presumption of substitutability") to accept Christianity is more rational than to reject it. In *Faith and Reason* (1981), Swinburne puts it this way: "If a man's religious inquiries lead him to believe that it is more probable that the Christian creed is true than that any rival creed is true, and he chooses to pursue the goals of religion he will be exercising Christian faith" (199).[11]

Key to Swinburne's argument is his discussion of five kinds or levels of rationality. A rational$_1$ belief is one that coheres with what else the holder believes (45). A belief that is inconsistent with what the holder believes is irrational$_1$.[12] A rational$_2$ belief is one grounded in proper basic beliefs (46). A belief that is based on basic beliefs which are held with confidence exceeding their probability or developed from basic beliefs by using faulty warrants is irrational$_2$. "A man must believe that his own beliefs are not merely rational$_1$, but rational$_2$" (48). A rational$_3$ belief is one that is rational$_2$ and whose supporting evidence and warrants have been checked to a degree viewed as adequate by the holder (49), given the importance of the issue, the level of probability of the belief, the expectation that an investigation will be useful, and the time the holder has available for investigation (53). An irrational$_3$ belief is one for which the holder has, culpably or not, failed to check the evidence and warrants adequately. A rational$_4$ belief is one that is rational$_3$ and which has been checked in a manner congruent with the holder's usual standards. A rational$_4$ belief is one held by a consistently reasonable person. A belief is irrational$_4$ if the holder has, consciously or not, failed to apply the usual standards in this case. The person is not being consistent. A rational$_5$ belief is one which is rational$_4$ and the holder's standards for evidence and warrants conform to "really adequate investigative procedures" (54). A belief is irrational$_5$ if it is subjectively adequate, but objectively inadequate. "If it matters that we have true beliefs, we must seek . . . rational$_5$ beliefs," (73) including rational$_5$ religious beliefs. A person with only rational$_5$ beliefs would be a fully rational person.

Swinburne asserts that calculations of probability provide a good inductive argument for the existence of God, that the evidence in the world is better explained accepting the hypothesis of theism than rejecting it. Thus, theism has a probability greater than 0.5 (1979:278). He, therefore, finds theism to be rational$_5$.

But what are the "really adequate investigative procedures" for exploring ultimate claims? The concept of adequate canons of evidence and inference is essentially contested. For example, Swinburne's construal of the canon of simplicity (1979:282) is opposed by Harry V. Stopes-Roe's argument that theism is not as simple a hypothesis as metaphysical naturalism, has no more real explanatory power, and therefore should not be preferred (Stopes-Roe 1977:44–71).[13] In short, the criteria by which rational$_5$ ultimate beliefs are to be established are essentially contested. Consequently, ultimate beliefs cannot be shown to be either rational$_5$ or irrational$_5$. Thus, Swinburne's attempt to show that theism is rational$_5$ is not successful because the attempt requires the use of unestablished criteria. He fails to construct a negative parity argument.

Nor is it clear that calculating the probability of theism is the right approach. No specific level of probability makes a belief rational. George Mavrodes (1986) has argued that although "probability beliefs may be reasons or causes for substantive beliefs, they are not identical with those beliefs, and the relation between them is not invariant" (210). Another issue is at what level of probability one should accept or reject a proposition. Again, Mavrodes (1982) has argued that the common sense notion that one should believe a proposition if the evidence shows it to have a probability greater than 0.5 is unsupported (64).[14] This natural, intuitive guide does not always provide the proper "threshold" for accepting or rejecting a proposition, nor for acting on that proposition. The theist might find, for instance, that the probability of a person being raised from the dead is highly improbable (at least on one construal of the evidence), and still might accept it as true. Finally, it is not clear whether Bayes' theorem, which Swinburne employs to calculate probabilities, can be used to indicate the probability of a single occurrence of a type of event. The universe began (if it began) once; it is not clear how to weigh the probabilities of its beginning or its initial development despite the claims of supporters of the anthropic principle.

If this analysis is correct, then a very sophisticated contemporary attempt to show theism more probable than other ultimate beliefs does not succeed. What Swinburne does show, however, is that theism can be rational$_4$. However, this conclusion leaves theism in a *permissive* parity position, for atheism can also be rational$_4$; and it certainly does not resolve the Penelhum's theological problem. Swinburne's attempt to determine the probability of theistic belief does not solve the problem of intellectual ambiguity, but shows how deep the problem is.

One root of this stalemate between Christian theism and atheism may in part result from a narrow focus on the rationality of beliefs. In this context, considering that a system of beliefs is the proper object of analysis will exclude some systems as irrational, but leave many to be rational. But because a belief is "irrational" in Swinburne's sense does not necessarily mean that the person holding it is irrational. For instance, a belief that p may be irrational, as Swinburne claims, if it contradicts other beliefs q, r, s, that a person holds. But such inconsistency does not mean that a *person* is irrational in *holding* all four. For instance, if s entails q and *not-p*, and Jane believes p, q, r, and s, it is not clear what she, as a rational person, should do. It may be rational for her to hold all four until further analysis shows them consistent, or until some minimal revision in their content makes them consistent, or until further investigation shows whether she should drop *p* or drop *s* (when dropping *s* may also undermine her belief *q* as well). However, it would seem irrational for someone, who holds *s*, which entails *not-p*, to *adopt* a belief that *p*. It is important to distinguish between both the rationality of holding and adopting beliefs, and the rationality of persons and of beliefs.

Alvin Plantinga has constructed a new version of a negative parity argument. He argues that, given the best argument for a naturalized epistemology, metaphysical naturalists or agnostics are in a position rationally inferior to theists. Rather than center, as Swinburne did, on the rationality of beliefs, Plantinga focuses on the rationality of persons. Again, given the principle of substitutability, this approach must be discussed for, if successful, it would go far to dissolving the appearance that theism and atheism are on an epistemic par.

A NEW DESIGN ARGUMENT FOR THE
REASONABLENESS OF BELIEVING IN GOD

In western philosophical traditions, the mainstream has answered the question, "What is knowledge?" by explicating three components. First, knowledge is *belief*. If I know that Jim is in the next room, I certainly believe it; but I may believe Jim is in the next room and not know it. Second, the belief must be *true* to count as knowledge. I can't straightforwardly think both that I know that Lisbon is in Portugal and I know that it is false that Lisbon is in Portugal. Something's wrong there. But a third component is needed, for not all true beliefs count as knowledge. I may believe (for whatever reason) that Dorothy Day will be canonized a saint within my lifetime and it may be true that she is canonized before I die, but that doesn't make my present belief, though true, knowledge. Something is missing. The third "missing" element is usually labeled "justification" (thus, knowledge equals justified, true, belief) or "warrant" or (occasionally) something else. One part of the story of Western philosophy is the debate over the nature of this third element.

Two basic patterns have emerged. The mainstream modern epistemological pattern is "internalist." For internalists, the descriptive question of how one acquires one's beliefs is less important than normative questions about whether (in general) we ought to use one or another method to acquire beliefs and if (in particular) I have dutifully and conscientiously used a proper method to form my belief. If I have used a good procedure properly, I have done my epistemic duty, and so my belief can be said to be (more or less) "justified." Each knower can, through introspection, determine the basis for his or her beliefs. Thus, an internal introspection can show whether a belief is "justified." Internalist epistemologists argue about what fulfilling one's epistemic duty is and what one has to do to make true belief knowledge. But in general, the third element can be called "justification."

Epistemic internalists tend to presume or argue that each of us has an epistemic *duty* to have justification for our beliefs. Debates in modern epistemology often tend to take this obligation for granted. It seems commonsensical, just as it makes sense to us that juries in the American jurisprudential system must find a person guilty only if the guilt is established "beyond reasonable doubt," or that entitlement to real estate is established only when a thorough search of the title records has been undertaken. If we cannot find or give our justification for our beliefs, we cannot be said to know them, only to believe in them.

The other modern pattern is "externalist." Laying claim to a heritage which goes back through the eighteenth-century Scottish common sense philosopher Thomas Reid to St. Thomas Aquinas and Aristotle, this pattern is a form of "naturalized epistemology." The actual belief-acquiring processes in which we "naturally" engage are taken to be reliable and proper generators of true beliefs. Indeed, arguments which pretend to show them unreliable tend, paradoxically and self-defeatingly, to rely on them. If I engage properly in a reliable practice or if my belief-acquiring faculties are functioning properly in an environment to which they are suited, then the beliefs I generate can be said to be "warranted." Externalism has no requirement that a person be able to introspect some condition that confers justification. I can know without knowing that I know or being able to show that I know. Rather, whether I know it or can find it out, my belief is warranted if and only if it is properly developed by my cognitive faculties working properly in a congenial environment. The appropriate use of a properly functioning memory, a well-constructed argument, or reliable testimony, etc., is the appropriate use of our belief-generating faculties which give us the warrant, the "third element," which makes true belief be knowledge. If my true belief is warranted, then I know it.

Externalists question whether any account of epistemic duty or appeal to "knowing that one knows" is needed in the account of the "third element." When Ptolemy espied the skies and formed a geocentric theory of the world, he used his properly functioning faculties of observation, inference, and analysis, among others, in an environment in which they naturally work quite well. His belief that the sun moved around the earth was, for him, warranted. It was not knowledge for him (although he evidently thought it was) because his belief was not true. And it is not knowledge for us not only because it is not true, but also because its warrant has been undermined or defeated by observations, inferences, and analyses that were not available to Ptolemy and which warrant a very different view of the universe. Its defeat is not Ptolemy's fault; after all, he didn't have Steven Hawking's faculties or facilities. If contemporary cosmologists generate a Theory of Everything, presumably it will be warranted unless defeated, and if it is a true belief, it will be knowledge (although we, like Ptolemy, might not know whether we know or whether we are only warranted to believe it—a *prima facie* oddity in reliabilist accounts of knowing).

Much of Plantinga (1993a) is an argument that the various modern forms of internalism hold "no real promise for a correct account of warrant" (vii) and, thus, a correct account of knowledge. In fact, there are many things I know without being able to introspect the conditions that make me warranted or justified in believing them. I certainly can't introspect the conditions that justify my belief that I am not a victim of an evil demon (or by monsters from outer space or by crazy scientists who have placed my brain in a vat and fed it carefully planned electrical stimuli). Such victimizing forces might be tricking me into merely imagining and falsely believing that I am typing this sentence into an old and slow computer on my office desk. If it is true that I am such a victim, my faculties are either malfunctioning terribly or have been placed into an environment in which they cannot function properly. In either case, there is no way I could justify (in an internalist sense) my belief that I am not such a victim (or that I am), since either my faculties aren't working right or they're working in an environment designed to deceive me. Yet I am surely warranted in my belief that I am typing this sentence into my old and slow computer, even if I cannot be justified in believing it. And if my belief about what I am doing is also true, then I do know it, even if I cannot give an account of why I am justified or even if I am not fully justified in believing it.[15]

Plantinga's arguments against the varieties of internalist epistemology and for an externalist account of warrant are far more subtle, extensive, and plausible than such a homely and brief account suggests. Given that epistemic naturalism is in the ascendent philosophically, Plantinga builds a strong case for taking "warrant" to be the "third element" in knowledge. As he puts it: "Being produced by properly functioning faculties aimed at truth in the environment for which those faculties are designed—these are central aspects of our concept of warrant" (1993a:214). For Plantinga, the key is not merely that our faculties are reliable (for they might be reliable by accident), but that they are properly functioning. To be properly functioning, our faculties must have a good design to explain why they do reliably (for the most part) aim at truth.

Yet there is a tremendous lacuna in many externalist accounts of knowing: how is it that the "design" is good, that the faculties *are* (mostly) reliable and functioning properly when we form true beliefs? If there is no answer to that question, then one cannot warrant the claim that there is a connection between warrant and truth. A reliabilist epistemology must presume that there is such a connection. But is there anything that shows the connection? Is there anything that makes the design of our faculties good? Is there any good reason to think that our faculties reliably aim at truth? Or is reliability simply an unwarranted assumption, a convenient postulate of naturalist epistemology?

Plantinga's arguments (1993b) are rather technical and complex—and involve extensive analysis of our cognitive faculties. But I think we can rough in a fairly nontechnical sketch of the part of his argument that is relevant to the present inquiry. We can begin by taking it for granted that our cognitive processes are roughly a result of whatever evolutionary forces made us capable of having and using complex belief-forming processes that yield large, articulated webs of beliefs. Most of these beliefs are also likely true. Our faculties usually function properly and generate true beliefs.

Given such reliability, the question Plantinga addresses is whether it can be accounted for on the thoroughly materialistic view which claims that evolution "has no mind and no mind's eye. It does not plan for the future. It has no vision, no foresight, no sight at all. If it can be said to play the role of watchmaker in nature, it is the *blind* watchmaker" (Dawkins 1986:5 as cited in Plantinga 1993b:197). Plantinga puts the question this way:

> It looks initially as if the notion of proper function *entails* that of design, so that necessarily, anything that functions properly has a design plan. And it also looks as if necessarily, if a thing has a design plan, then either that thing or some ancestor of it was designed by a rational being. The real question is whether these appearances are deceiving; the real question is whether there is a satisfactory *naturalistic* explanation of the notion of proper function (1993b:198).

His answer is that there is not.

The problem seems to be that metaphysical naturalists (or materialists) have, as one naturalist put it, to explain "How could consciousness arise in a purely material universe? How could minds be made out of matter? This difficulty for materialist and naturalist views has been stressed repeatedly and in various forms" (Mackie 1982:119). It is forcefully made clear in a recent essay in which Thomas Nagel (1993) endorses John R. Searle's (1992) contention that

> materialists are drawn to implausible forms of psychophysical reduction because they assume that if mental states cannot be explained in such terms, then the inescapable alternative is dualism: they would then have to admit that nonphysical substances or properties are basic features of reality. And the fear of dualism, with its religious and spiritualist and otherwise unscientific associations, drives them to embrace reductionist materialism at any intellectual cost (1993:38).

Nagel identifies himself as a proponent of the

> "dual aspect theory," to express the view deriving from Spinoza that mental phenomena are the subjective aspects of states which can also be described physically. But all I would claim for the idea is that it is somewhat less unacceptable than the other unacceptable theories currently on offer. I share Searle's aversion to both dualism and materialism, and believe a solution to the mind-body problem is nowhere in sight (1993:40).

So far it seems as though the argument is following a well-known path that will lead to the familiar dead end of a permissive parity position. As Robert Merrihew Adams (1987) once put it, given the cost of reductionist materialism and given that the "dual aspect theory" has no way of explaining how or why mental and physical states or aspects are correlated, a better path should be followed: "Theism seems a less desperate expedient" (260). But if there is no solution to the mind-body problem in sight for materialists, there is also no solution to the problem of evil in sight for theists. Each position has some explanatory power, but each leaves the relationships between some important aspects of reality unexplained.[16] Unless one thinks that it is far more important to solve the mind-body problem using theism despite the problem of evil, or to leave the mind-body problem unresolved if the cost of solving it is dualism in some form (most of which open the door for metaphysical theism to return), one should probably find that naturalism and theism seem roughly on an epistemic par.

Plantinga, however, intensifies the problem for the naturalist. First, he borrows an argument from Stich (1990) to show that "it is perfectly possible both that we and our cognitive faculties have evolved in the ways approved by current evolutionary theory, and that those cognitive faculties are not reliable" (1993b:222). This argument seems practically incontestable.

Second, he asks what is the probability that our cognitive faculties are reliable if our faculties have developed by evolution and that evolution is blind (as Dawkins [1986] claims). Plantinga's answer to this question involves a complex argument (which even he admits uses only "vague estimates" [1993b:228] of probabilities in analyzing the possible options) to reach his conclusion that the probability is rather low. One may say that the probability of such an occurrence would require amazing luck or fortunate chance—events of low probability.

Plantinga's argument runs roughly like this: Presume you are committed to our having cognitive faculties, to evolution as the process by which they develop, and to naturalism, that is, that evolution is a purely natural process, as Dawkins put it. Say you assign these views probabilities of 100%, 90% and 95% respectively. The probability that results is 86%, a rather high probability. The only other factor not included here is the reliability of our faculties. To reach, then, the conclusion that the probability that naturalistic (95%) evolution (90%) yielded cognitive faculties (100%) that are reliable (x%) is rather low—

say 40% to be generous—you need to solve for x, and you'd actually get a result of about 34%.

Plantinga's point is that if you believe our having cognitive faculties is certain, naturalism is nearly certain, and evolution by natural selection, genetic drift, random walk, or similar event is highly likely, then you have to agree that your claim that our cognitive faculties are mostly reliable has a rather low probability. Therefore, you have good reason to doubt the reliability of your cognitive faculties (especially at the rarefied level of complex theory). But it is just those cognitive faculties which devised the theory of naturalistic evolution! Yet these faculties must have a low reliability. Thus, you are in the unenviable position of claiming that you have developed a highly reliable theory with rather unreliable cognitive faculties!

Third, Plantinga notes that the theist is not in such an appalling position (see 1993b:236). The theist can recognize that we have cognitive faculties, that they are mostly reliable for producing true beliefs (which may be a condition for human thriving that is improbable on the naturalists' views), and that in some way God guides evolution so that free humans with reliable cognitive faculties will emerge. Now theism still has no *explanation* of the problem of evil, but theists can show that the reality of evil does not necessarily or even probably count against the existence of God. So theists are in the enviable position of having an explanation that allows them to account for the reliable character of our cognitive faculties—God brought it about that they function well, that they are well-designed.

What Plantinga has developed here is a negative parity argument. The naturalist epistemologist who is also a metaphysical naturalist is tied up in knots. The naturalist epistemologist who is a supernaturalist in metaphysics is not. If it is successful, Plantinga has shown that supernaturalism is a better explanation of the contemporary dominant form of epistemology than naturalism. In this case, he has created an argument that goes substantially beyond Swinburne's or any other argument from design to the reality of God. "Naturalistic epistemology conjoined with naturalistic metaphysics leads *via* evolution to . . . violation of canons of rationality; conjoined with theism it does not. The naturalistic epistemologist should therefore prefer theism to metaphysical naturalism" (1993b:237).[17] If Plantinga is correct, theism has far more explanatory power for the naturalist, reliabilist epistemologist than materialism.

Has Plantinga formulated a new argument that can prove the existence of God from the design of the world? The best answer at this point is "perhaps." Not all epistemologists accept his arguments against epistemic internalism (remember his argument applies only for those who are externalists). Thus, Linda Zagzebski (1993) finds that Plantinga's argument leads to the claim that theists must be blessed with incredible good luck and nontheists with bad luck, a position that is philosophically unsatisfactory (202), even if it can find some support in theological theories of grace. This outcome is the *prima facie* oddity I noted above; but it applies not only to atheists or agnostics, but seems a characteristic of all human knowing.

Zagzebski also finds that Plantinga's account has no room for the social components of knowledge or an account of epistemic virtue. As she puts it:

> From what has been said so far, I conclude that knowledge is not only the possession of true beliefs but also the possession of them in an admirable way that comes from either an instinct or an intellectual habit worthy of our aspiration. Such a habit is in part a process that reliably leads to truth. This process must also be generated by a certain motive—briefly, a passion for truth (1993:216).

One of the virtues that knowers need to develop is what Aristotle called *phronesis*, according to Zagzebski, which is neither rule-governed nor easy to portray (215–16), but essential in the practical-intellectual life. If Zagzebski is correct (and I think she is), then an individualistic naturalism like Plantinga's at least needs supplementation to avoid an appeal to luck or grace as necessary elements in epistemology and to account for the fact that we learn how to know by learning practices—a necessarily social account. Even if modern internalists cannot find a satisfactory account of the "third element" in knowledge, perhaps other accounts can be found which avoid the oddity that we don't know when we know (see also Greco 1993:176–78). If a better account of knowing is found, one that is not so thoroughly "externalist" and "individualist" as Plantinga's, then his argument may become irrelevant or require modification.

Some may question the applicability of the calculation of probabilities in this context, arguing that it works only where one has larger statistical samples and that the estimates are so rough as to be practically meaningless. Others may say that Plantinga has failed to differentiate higher from lower cognitive faculties and that doing so might not create the problems he finds endemic for the thoroughgoing naturalist—and, as Zagzebski notes, might not be so easily explained as he thinks. And given the checkered history of design arguments, one may think that the likelihood that his will succeed as a *negative* parity argument is rather low.

Let's assume, however, that Plantinga's argument is a success. At what has he succeeded? He has shown that metaphysical naturalism is inferior to metaphysical supernaturalism as an explanatory hypothesis for epistemological naturalists. He points out that traditional Jewish, Muslim, or Christian theists are thus in better shape than materialists if epistemological naturalism is true. But so are those, who believe that a very powerful and possibly very wise and possibly very good being has made humanity, in better shape than materialists. So might many others who have different views of the supernatural have accounts that are better for epistemological naturalists than materialism is. What he has not shown is whether there is a *best* explanation of the evidence and whether theism is that explanation. Given the reality of religious diversity and the diversity of metaphysical beliefs that are not materialistic, Plantinga, like the other defensive philosophers of religion criticized in chapter 1, makes an argument against the cultured despisers of religion, but one that fails to take us far in discerning among various religious commitments. Plantinga would respond, of course, that such discernment wasn't his point; but that is precisely the problem—the real point of making religious commitments (or avoiding them) is obscured. Other traditions have the resources to develop nontheistic or nonmonotheistic explanations of "design," so the practical problem remains unsolved, even obscured.

Plantinga, unlike some epistemologists, does not take on the disembodied subject; he is an explicitly committed Christian philosopher; his opponent has a social and intellectual location as an intellectual agnostic or materialist of the contemporary academy. But nonetheless the issues he treats are far from those facing a person who lives in a world of profound religious conflict, who is shaped by a religious tradition, but who also finds other traditions attractive, and who seeks to make a wise commitment. Plantinga remains within the dominant tradition in modern philosophy of religion, arguing with the best academic minds that Jewish, Christian and Muslim theisms are not defeated as explanations. But if you are a young African-

American, raised a Baptist and proselytized and attracted by the Nation of Islam, all this would seem rather academic. Plantinga might say that this dilemma is not material for philosophy of religion, but for pastoral care (compare Plantinga 1974:28). But from the perspective of a practical philosophy of religion, this construal of philosophy of religion is just the problem. The academic issues regarding rational theology and metaphysical preferences are interesting to academics and are of great use for the exploration of rational theology—a point that theologians should not overlook. But if philosophy of religion is simply rational theology, then it ignores the issues that affect religious practice and belief. More is needed.

Our third epistemologist attends more closely to how actual religious practices shape beliefs. In recent years, philosophers of religion in general and religious epistemologists in particular have become more sensitive to the fact that religious beliefs cannot be abstracted from religious practices and traditions. Numerous authors (Katz [1978] and Lash [1988] among others) have recognized the role religious traditions play in forming religious beliefs. In the works of William P. Alston, we find a pattern that takes us away from propositions that express a better explanation of a philosophical account and into religious practices and the beliefs they generate.

A PRACTICAL APPROACH TO JUSTIFYING RELIGIOUS BELIEF

In an elegant and complex argument Alston construes warranted religious beliefs as generated in a reliable religious practice, thus avoiding the severing of religious beliefs from religious practice and focusing on the reasonableness of persons, rather than the rationality of beliefs. Here I will argue that even Alston's philosophy suffers from a truncated view of religion that undermines his conclusions. Nevertheless, Alston clearly sets religious epistemology on the right path as he returns, finally, to the practices of religion and to construing the key issues as practical issues.

Alston's purpose is to show that it is rational for someone to participate in what he calls Christian Mystical Practice (CMP) because CMP "is a socially established doxastic practice that is not demonstrably unreliable or otherwise disqualified for rational acceptance" (1991:194) and to hold beliefs which that participation reliably generates. Alston's epistemology, like Plantinga's, is a form of epistemic naturalism. But Alston focuses not on our faculties and the theories that account for them, but on religious practice in particular. Once Alston's approach is confronted with actual practices, however, CMP splinters into multiple practices and a central part of his contribution is undermined. A more complete account requires a richer understanding of religious diversity and a more precise account of religious practices than Alston acknowledges.

Alston begins by analyzing mystics' reports and arguing that there are no sound arguments against their claim that they directly perceive God or even against the more common believers' "mystical" claims that they perceive God in various ways. Mystical beliefs, like perceptual beliefs, are based on experiences plus associated background beliefs: just as my belief, "what appears to me as yellow is yellow," requires not only a bare perceptual input, but also the ability to use background color concepts, so a mystic's belief "what appears to me as God is God," requires not only a bare mystical input, but also the ability to use background theological concepts. Background beliefs are ingredients in perceptual and mystical experience.

The question is whether mystical practice renders mystical beliefs rationally justified. Alston argues that if beliefs are formed in a reliable practice, they are *prima facie* justified. Crucially, he claims that only circular arguments can be found to show the reliability either of the common practice of forming perceptual beliefs (PP) or CMP. Save that the former is practically universal and the latter more limited, they are practically on an epistemic par in terms of reliability. Moreover, each practice has a system of "overriders" or "checks" that weed out unjustified beliefs when doubts about specific beliefs arise (1991:79).

In Alston's account, overriders are that part of a doxastic practice which weeds out unjustified beliefs developed by engaging in the practice. These overriders vary from practice to practice; what counts as an overrider in a tort law or in chicken sexing may not count in astrophysics. Unless an overrider obtains, it is rational to accept as *prima facie* (at least) justified those beliefs formed by properly engaging in a reliable practice. Just as I am justified in believing that the "Post-It Note" in front of me *is* yellow unless the room is bathed in yellow light, or I have jaundice, etc., so mystics are justified in believing that what appears to them as God *is* God unless the devil counterfeits the experience, or they are hallucinating, etc.

Notice that Alston's account is a modified or impure form of epistemological externalism.[18] He claims that a perceptual or a mystical perceiver is justified if defeating conditions do not obtain, not by the perceiver's ability to *know* or *show* that defeating conditions do not obtain. Yet discovering that a relevant defeating condition obtains could "override" the individual's being justified in holding the specific perceptual or mystical belief. Such a discovery would not, however, "undermine" the *practice* of forming either perceptual or mystical beliefs. Specific beliefs may fall, but socially established doxastic practices remain standing because the overriders are internal to the practice.

Alston argues that opponents who try to show that participating in CMP is less rational than participating in PP either apply a double standard or engage in epistemic imperialism (applying standards from one practice willy-nilly to another). He works to undermine arguments which would show that CMP is unreliable. The most obvious one is that CMP should be disqualified because PP is universal and CMP is not. But scientific practice (SP) is not universal, and it is a paradigm of a reliable practice. Thus, the fact that a practice is not universal does not necessarily constitute a good argument against its reliability (a point that counts strongly against Flew and others who seem to think that only evidence which is rationally discoverable by "anyone" is permissible in argument). If our beliefs are formed in a reliable practice, then they are *prima facie* justified; CMP has not been shown to be less reliable than perceptual practice (only less widespread), so the beliefs formed in it are as *prima facie* justified as beliefs formed in perceptual practice.

Because mystical practices in different religious traditions have different background beliefs and overrider systems, they are irreducibly different, not a single practice with multiple variations. Alston must thus address the sticky problem of the multiplicity of religions. He concludes that although the multiplicity of mystical practices renders CMP epistemically weaker than PP, if there are no "external reasons for supposing that one of the competing practices is more accurate than my own, the only rational course for me is to sit tight with the practice of which I am a master and which serves me so well in guiding my activity in the world" (1991:274). One can reasonably hope and perhaps even work for a time when "inter-practice contradictions will be sorted out" (1991:7), but that is not relevant to my being justified now in holding that it is rational to think CMP is epistemically reliable and in holding beliefs that I develop while participating in CMP. In effect, Alston's account of religious pluralism reaches a conclusion very similar to Plantinga's: the believer's position is undefeated and thus the believer is warranted in keeping her or his position.

Alston's practical approach has great strengths. For instance, he offers a clear and nuanced account of the way traditions shape beliefs. In common with other belief-forming practices, such as the practice of forming beliefs about perceptions, our religious beliefs are based on present experience interpreted in the context of background beliefs. Background beliefs do not cause the experience. Rather, they provide the language necessary for identifying and understanding the experience and communicating the belief developed. They are ingredients in, but neither bases for nor interpretations of, perceptual and mystical experience.[19]

Moreover, Alston's account has room for epistemic virtues (although he does not make much of them). If we learn how to form beliefs by engaging in practices, our models are those who have learned the practice very well. These paragons of ability may come by it "naturally"; they may be gifted as some athletes are. But even gifted athletes, not to mention gifted knowers, need to learn how to use their gifts well. In so doing, they can become models for exercising the practices in which they excel.

However, Alston's neglect of the role of institutional components in the overrider systems of doxastic practices leads to a central difficulty in his work. The institutional element of religion is, as I argued in chapter 2, a necessary element in religion. But Alston ignores the ways institutions shape belief and does not recognize the institutional components in overrider systems. His dilemma is this: either the practice he wishes to defend, CMP, is one of many Christian practices or it is nonexistent. If the former, Alston does not show that CMP is preferable to other practices; if the latter, the argument needs substantial revision.

Alston characterizes the overrider system of CMP as follows: "CMP takes the Bible, the ecumenical councils of the undivided church, Christian experience through the ages, Christian thought, and more generally the Christian tradition as normative sources of its overrider system." He recognizes that there are problem "borderline areas. If we try to precise the concept too much we end up with an unmanageable plurality of practices" (1991:193). But if we "precise" the concept too little, we will fail to describe any practice with sufficient accuracy to identify it at all.

The fact is that a substantial number of Christian communities would accept far fewer or far more constituents in their overrider systems. The various Christian communities do have substantially different overrider systems, which Alston fails to acknowledge. There is, alas, what he calls an "unmanageable" plurality of irreducible practices within Christianity.

The key to Alston's problem is that he cites only *resources* for constituting an overrider system for CMP; but an overrider system requires not merely resources, but also *mechanisms, procedures*, and *authorities*. His "resources" are part of the tradition, part of the background beliefs that many Christians share, but the mechanisms and procedures for overriding specific beliefs are institutionalized rather differently in the various forms of Christianity. Alston fails to distinguish three distinguishable elements in a religion: tradition, community, and institution. As I noted in chapter 2, traditions provide resources for the practices and beliefs of the adherents of religions; institutions preserve traditions by keeping them available through time; communities dwell in traditions and are usually supported and often girded by institutional authorities.

Now Alston has shown that the criteria of one doxastic practice need not apply to the others. But in each of the practices there are procedures for checking and authorities whose competence is acknowledged. In nonuniversal practices, institutional status is a factor in determining who has an authoritative say within the community of participants in the practice. Resources drawn from a tradition of practice alone are not sufficient to constitute an overrider system in any practice; they are the presuppositions of a practical overrider system.

Consider a different nonuniversal doxastic practice: experimental physics. In the community of physicists, duplication of results is crucial; it is finally why scientists refused to countenance the "discovery" of "cold fusion" and accepted the discovery of "(relatively) high-temperature superconductivity." No direct appeal is made to resources. They are presumed. The *procedure* of duplication provides the criterion for acceptance; if an experiment can be independently duplicated, its results are accepted. The mechanisms and processes are clear because they are institutionalized in the community that engages in SP.

Who are the physicists' authorities? The community of competent physicists is taken as appropriate to determine whether experimental claims are overridden. And membership in that community is established, for better or worse, in part, by the fact that the "experts" have institutional support and roles that establish their expertise. They have developed intellectual virtues which are recognized by their peers. They have university and research institute appointments. They publish results in journals respected in their field. Roughly speaking, the prestige of their appointments mirrors their authority. A physicist without a recognized lab is not recognized as an authority in the community. Results of experiments published in *Modern Theology* would not be taken seriously. To neglect the institutional basis and communal exercise of scientific authority is to misconstrue the actual practice of science.

Other doxastic practices also have mechanisms and authorities: consider literary and aesthetic evaluation, examining doctoral dissertations in the humanities, or deciding whether logging in a certain area will destroy the habitat of an endangered species, etc. All of these are belief-forming practices. In fact, perceptual practice is one of the few practices in which institutional status is irrelevant to participating in the community that functions as an authoritative body for judging claims generated in the practice. Perception is a (practically) universal practice. Although it has its experts and its incompetents, its Sherlocks and its Watsons, institutional status is generally irrelevant to authoritative status. Had Alston taken other practices as "local" or as nonuniversal as CMP for his epistemic analogues, the institutional components in them and the analogues in religious practices might have been clearer. But when one considers the nearly universal practice of perception as an analogue to CMP (rather than other, more "exclusive" practices) the crucial institutional component is effaced.

Alston does not notice that while mainstream Christian mystical practices share resources for their overrider systems, they do not share procedures, mechanisms, or authorities. Nor do all Christians give the same weight or relative priority to the resources Alston cites. Nor can they be said to be members of the same community, shaped by the same tradition. Fundamentalists claim to rely almost exclusively on the biblical text; Roman Catholics appeal to tradition more heavily than Baptists. Individual experience may count far more for communities of "born-again Christians" than for those less charismatically focused. What makes Christian practices seem so similar is this overlapping of resources for overrider systems, not their actual overrider systems.

Significant differences in overrider systems differentiate doxastic practices. These differences allow Alston to find Buddhist mysticism a practice different from Christian mysticism. But if there are significant differences in overrider systems among the various Christian denominational groups as well, then "Christian mystical practice" must also be multiple. Each Christian institution has different mechanisms for dealing with those who generate and proclaim beliefs not consonant with the traditional beliefs the institution defends and transmits. Roman Catholics authorities can excommunicate; Mennonite communities can shun. On Alston's account, as "mystical practice" in general cannot be construed as a single practice with local variations, so "Christian mystical practice" cannot be a single doxastic practice. There may also be families of mystical practices between religious traditions, for example, absorptive practices and unitive practices, among others.

More to the point, there are families of mystical practices within Christianity, but either CMP is too vague to pick out all of them or CMP is merely one of those practices in the family. By ignoring the institutional element, Alston is covertly proposing "Christian individualist mystical practice" as his prime example (which ignores institutional authority in an overrider system and makes each individual the final judge). Alston (1994) rejects this point and claims his work has room for the institutional element of religion, but the importance of the institution remains (at best) profoundly underdeveloped in his work. As I have argued elsewhere (1992), Alston's approach finally gets us no further than William James's (1902) individualistic claims about the reliability of religious experience, which is not very far.

Moreover, Alston does not adequately consider how social location shapes religious practices. The kind of doxastic practices developed differ profoundly in rural *communidades de base*, in vibrant North American Catholic parishes, in underground Baptist communities grown up under persecuting political systems, in Womenchurch gatherings, and in nineteenth-century American Methodist Episcopal Zionist communities, for example. The concrete communities in which an embodied person develops CMP are obscured, notwithstanding that the actual beliefs developed in such differing communities can differ wildly. For example, members of each of these communities will typically develop rather different concepts of liberation, salvation, or redemption, that is, of the ways in which what is crooked in the world can be construed and straightened. Alston might say that to consider such diversity would make for unmanageable plurality. But perhaps unity is not a solution to the problem of understanding religious believing, but part of the problem; perhaps smoothing out such diversity makes for too much simplicity.

In this sense, the members of the Branch Davidian cult who died in Waco, Texas, in 1993 could all (except possibly David Koresh) be warranted in believing in Koresh on Alston's account. Perhaps, from some Christian or more general epistemic perspective, the Waco Branch Davidians failed to use the resources of the tradition as overriders, but if the charismatically powerful leader rejects those overriders (and any external institutional control), then there is no clear violation of epistemic propriety or obligation on Alston's account. Indeed, if one accepts John Hick's claim that in a situation of theoretical ambiguity, one may trust one's "religious experience and to be prompted by it to trust one of the great religious figures" (Hick 1989:228), then Koresh's followers were about as warranted as they could be in following Koresh. Whether the Waco group can successfully be used in a *reductio ad absurdum* argument against the dominant pattern in religious epistemology remains to be seen, but the possibility is there: they seem to be the sort of theists that Plantinga and Alston would have to find warranted in their beliefs.

As the example of the Branch Davidians shows in practice, CMP is multiple. Alston can make "mainstream CMP" appear to be a unified practice only because he focuses on the resources and neglects to focus on the mechanisms and institutional authorities constitutive of effective overrider systems. But once the variations in the processes of overriding are surfaced, and one sees that what counts as an overriding for a devout Catholic does not count for a devout Quaker or Methodist or (Koreshian) Branch Davidian, then one sees that the overriding systems are sufficiently different to require the balkanization of Christian mystical practices.

Now Alston can easily reply that he is not writing in the "comparative study of religions but in the epistemology of religious experience and belief. From that standpoint any practice is brought in only as an illustration of general philosophical points" (1991:192–93). But confronting his account with actual religious practices and showing that his account fails to portray the variety of overrider systems adequately shows that his account requires substantial amendment to be adequate to pick out and describe the diversity of irreducible doxastic practices within the Christian traditions, much less between traditions.

The result of inattention to mechanisms of overriding seems to be an ultraliberal account wherein each individual must judge for oneself whether one's beliefs are in line with the tradition's resources. But that is hardly mainstream Christian mystical practice. Alston's work is clearly one very important step to a more adequate religious epistemology. But it remains an analysis of a practice which misconstrues many practices as if they were reducible to one. It thus covertly valorizes a single, liberal practice.

The problem of diversity in religious practices is obviously more acute than Alston's practical approach to religious epistemology allows. The problem of many practices with which we began in chapter 1 remains acute even on this approach to religious epistemology.

The problem has two aspects: first, the external problem of religious diversity. Alston argues that there is no practice-independent way of judging practices:

> The most fundamental stratum of my "doxastic practice" approach is the claim that there is no appeal beyond the doxastic practices to which we find ourselves firmly committed. That claim is based solely on the pervasiveness of epistemic circularity in attempts to show those practices to be reliable. The only reliance here is on reasoning, including rational intuition, something we perforce rely on in any intellectual activity whatever. It does not require any sociological or psychological investigation into the status SP and the like have in our personal and corporate lives. . . .
>
> The rest of my case . . . I have admitted to exhibit epistemic circularity and so to constitute "significant self-support" in a wider sense. Nevertheless my approach is still distinguished from the purely internal one by the fact that it involves a general reflection on doxastic practices and the vicissitudes of trying to show them to be reliable, an "external" perspective that is most prominent in what I call the basic stratum of the position—the thesis that there is no appeal beyond the doxastic practices with which we find ourselves (1991:177).

If that is so, and if CMP is not one practice, but many, then we are left with an epistemological position not merely analogous to, but indistinguishable from, a fideistic religious internalism (1991:180). Presumably, it would be rational for various people to participate not only in each of the Christian doxastic practices but also in numerous other religious practices because each has not been shown to be unreliable, a point Alston practically concedes (1991:276). Some may be comfortable with fideism, but a theoretical fideism has difficulty in differentiating worthwhile from worthless, but self-consistent, belief systems. In the aftermath of the Waco disaster, such fideism seems rationally undesirable and practically untenable.

However, there is also a second aspect of the problem of diversity that Alston does not consider, a problem of internal diversity. There arises in practice a dilemma of differentiating which overriding resources and mechanisms are *internal* to one's own practice. Alston argues plausibly that in the context of religious pluralism where numerous practices seem to be *prima facie* reliable, individuals are within their epistemic rights to remain within, to "sit tight" within, their own practice as long as it has not been shown, internally or externally, to be unreliable. One could even go further and suggest that this might be the prudent choice to make. But take, for example, Catholic Christians whose religious practices are based in Catholic Christian mystical traditions, but who also search other traditions as well. They want, perhaps, to find analogues to Catholic Christian practice and hope to generate insights into areas in which the Catholic tradition has had blind spots. Or suppose, for example, that a Catholic theologian develops a set of practices and generates a set of beliefs about the ways God is present in the creation that is dubbed "Creation Spirituality." Suppose also that these beliefs are found by Catholic authorities to fail to be in accord with the Roman Catholic tradition that has nurtured this theologian. The authorities' reading of the traditional resources leads them to the judgment that these beliefs—and perhaps even the practices that generate them—are not compatible with the tradition. The authorities then order the theologian (invoking, perhaps, a vow of obedience) to return to more traditional beliefs and practices. How can this theologian follow Alston's good advice to sit tight? Has a new practice developed or not? Should one sit tight in the practices that seem to be providing religious insights for many believers? Or should one sit tight in the Catholic practice that recognizes the authority of the institutional officers? In practice, should one resist or give in? We cannot answer that question because Alston's account fails to differentiate practices sufficiently. In short, Alston's account is not nuanced enough to show how his good advice might be followed in this concrete case. Without considering the institutional mechanisms,

Alstonian advice to "sit tight" within one's own practice and one's own tradition misfires because an Alstonian account omits the mechanisms of the overrider systems and thus cannot differentiate practices clearly. On Alston's account there is no way to tell if one is a "master" of traditional Catholic Christian practice or a "master" of a new practice.

When confronted with actual practices, Alston's approach fails to differentiate practices adequately and thus also to identify practices sufficiently. If the theologian's practice is part of the Catholic Christian tradition, then the condemned beliefs and practices should be abandoned. If the theologian's practice is not part of that tradition, then perhaps one should abandon the traditional practices and its authoritative overrider system and "sit tight with" one's own practice. But the only way to tell in which practice the theologian is engaging is to take account of the institutional authorities and their role which is internal to (and partly constitutive of) the overrider system of Catholic Christian mystical practice and external to (and perhaps irrelevant to) an overrider system of a different mystical practice, including those within other branches of Christianity. Only if the CMPs can be differentiated, can the Alstonian "sit tight" advice make sense. But on Alston's account as it stands, this differentiation cannot be done.[20]

Thus, a form of the experiential argument for the justification of religious belief has come to center stage. In its Plantingan and Alstonian forms, it does not provide an independent foundation for religious belief, but is a contextually shaped response to circumstances that trigger religious belief. However, its proponents, like many epistemologists of religion, construct an argument directed against the skeptics who would discount religious doxastic practices and the beliefs they generate. In this context, the resultant argument appears like fideism, which, along with foundationalism, is one of the two classic theological responses to skepticism. Although Alston attempts to work in the vein of naturalized epistemology associated with Reid, Newman, and Wittgenstein among others, his account remains more a defensive counter to skepticism than a philosophical analysis of religious knowing seeking to differentiate reliable from unreliable religious practices. He thus ignores a crucial problem: the way overrider systems function in practice to differentiate better from worse practices.

This defensiveness seems to be a general weakness of accounts that take religiously unsympathetic epistemologists as their primary dialogue partners: They leave us with insoluble dilemmas. They may

show that religious beliefs are, *pace* the cultured despisers, not irrational. Many traditions evidently yield relatively justified, but incompatible, experientially-based beliefs. Many traditions are impressive even
to nonparticipants. Many of them are not obviously incoherent, and
many have significant self-support. Arguments against religious practices are unwarrantedly imperialistic, seeking to colonize religious
practice with inappropriate overriders at home in other practices. But
defensive accounts leave those who are forced to choose with the
dilemma of having to choose on nonrational grounds among practices
that generate incompatible, but prima facie justified, beliefs for those
who participate in them.

Thus, religious diversity remains a problem that is even more
difficult to overcome than Alston thought. A thoroughgoing naturalized religious epistemology must examine more closely the social and
institutional matrices of religious practices, recognize that institutional
elements are internal to religious practices, and offer an account that
recognizes diversity as a problem internal to religious life. Many individuals are confronted with religious choices in our pluralistic age,
and Alston's epistemology has no clear place for dealing with this fact
as an epistemic issue—which it is for many. His epistemic naturalism is
a giant step in the right direction, but it has not reached the promised
land of providing a practical epistemology for justifying religious belief
in the context of the evidently irreducible pluralism in religious practices.

Most modern religious epistemologists are caught in a dilemma.
If the justifiability of belief in God entitled one to participate in a
religious tradition, then it seems that one is justified in participating
in any of the Western monotheisms, even the most vicious forms of
them (e.g., the German Christian Church during World War II, the
terrorist groups that form some of the Islamic Jihad movements in
the middle east today, the Branch Davidians of the Adventist family
of Christianity in Waco, Texas, Roman Catholicism, or Missouri Synod
Lutheranism, etc.). But if justifiability of belief in God has no *practical*
entailments or implications, then the justifiability of that belief is
finally empty of implications for participation in a religious tradition
or for the believers' life. In short, the epistemic entitlement to hold a
proposition like "God exists" has no clear relevance to religion as
practiced. Whichever path one takes, the modern focus on one's entitlement to believe in God ought hardly be a central issue in philosophy
of religion, even though it may be a key point in rational theology

and in the defense of belief against its assailants. A person's real dilemma *in vivo* is obscured by the religious epistemologists' analyses.

Perhaps the greatest problem of these analyses is their epistemic individualism and atomism, even in the improved approach Alston takes. The insights in these various approaches demand that we attend to them, despite our disagreements. Yet the problems they generate give us good reasons to try another approach, to focus on religion as a whole since examining religious belief as abstracted from religious traditions has come to a dead end to recognize that the issue is not one of religious belief, but of practice.[21] We need to solve Pascal's problem: into which practices will we put our bodies, ourselves. In short, after Swinburne, Plantinga, and Alston, our exemplars of modern religious epistemology, we must return to the Pascalian issue and try to resolve the problem of many practices.[22]

NOTES TO CHAPTER 3

1. Plantinga has promised a third volume to be entitled *Warranted Christian Belief* that should address these questions. But this title and the conclusion to 1993b suggest that his focus will remain on warranting theological beliefs abstracted from religious life and not venture into substantial discussion of religious diversity.

2. One might argue that the difference is in the morality or ethos of each tradition, and so the choice is not indifferent, but to be found in the moral realm. While that point may be true, it just moves the argument to a different set of beliefs. Controversies about basic moral principles or virtues are at least as insoluble rationally as religious controversies.

3. Examples of this tendency abound. For instance, numerous critics of Alvin Plantinga's "Free Will Defense" of the compatibility of belief in an omnipotent, omniscient, omnibenevolent God and that there is real evil in the actual world make this sort of error (see Tilley 1984:1991). When Richard Swinburne defends his definition of God by arguing for the possibility that there could be a person without a body, Flew makes this error when he accuses Swinburne of having an "unsound method. He insists on introducing imaginary puzzle cases . . . [to which] there may be no unequivocally correct answers to possible new questions about personal identity" (see Flew 1985: 113). Flew unfortunately mistakes the logic of Swinburne's argument at this point, for all Swinburne attempts to do is to show the *coherence* of the concept of God, not its credibility; at this point (although not at others), his argument is religiously "internalist" or quasi-internalist.

4. The analysis of Pascal's *Pensées* in chapter 1 suggests that his argument was not a "negative parity argument." Nonetheless, many mainstream philosophers of religion, especially consistent externalists, have thought that it would be the best argument one could find in *Pensées*. Deciding whether Pascal's argument is a sample of a negative parity argument is irrelevant to the issue of whether Penelhum analyzed the logic and rhetoric of such arguments correctly; I am persuaded that he did, even though I am not persuaded that Pascal's argument is a parity argument.

5. A properly basic belief is a belief that is not based on other beliefs or on argument or on inference, but is *basic* to (at the bottom or edge of) our system of beliefs, and it is proper in that a person is warranted in believing it (I believe that the woman I spot going into the door of my house is my wife, presuming that I am in good position to see her, my cognitive faculties are working well, and no conditions obtain to undermine or override my belief). See Tilley 1990:238–45, the literature cited there, and the next two sections of the present chapter.

6. See also Flew (1976). In "The Burden of Proof" (1985), Flew argues that he does not have to defend his procedure, but the issue is not his procedure, but his principles.

7. Although Nielsen can be seen as constructing a *negative* parity argument (1971, chapter 6), his attempts to defeat theism are far less successful than his attempt to ground ethics without resort to religious sanctions. For example, *Ethics Without God* (1973), relies primarily on a permissive parity argument for its cogency. I will not pursue these exegetical and historical points here.

8. This position contrasts with Nielsen's negative account of *ad hominem* arguments ten pages earlier, when these are undertaken by internalists.

9. A similar argument has been mounted by McCarthy (1982) to show that some contemporary liberal theologians (e.g., Hans Küng and Schubert Ogden), who claim that having the concept of a meaningful human life entails accepting a transcendent ground for that meaning, have not sustained their argument. These theologians seem to be trying (and failing) to construct *negative* parity arguments for their positions by arguing that an atheistic view is epistemically inferior because epistemically thwarted or incoherent. Rocca (1986) persuasively argues that Küng's position is finally "internalist" and fails to provide any warrant for his claim for a foundation of Christian faith in "basic trust." But if it can be understood as a "permissive parity argument," it also shows that opponents have not shown that the beliefs constitutive of Christian faith are irrational.

10. One might join Plantinga (1983:65–68, 89–90) and attribute unbelievers' reluctance to believe in God to sin. However, such a move may provide reason to exclude them from participating in a reasonable conversation. It may also show such religious belief imprudent, in terms to be discussed in chapter 5. Moreover, Plantinga's repeated responses to the frivolous "Great Pumpkin Objection," rather than to serious proposals from other traditions, obscure the possibility that non-Christian traditions might be as legitimate as Christian contexts are for developing basic beliefs.

11. Swinburne's language is unrelievedly and obnoxiously noninclusive. I will not note or correct it further. Tilley (1991:236–38) offers a possible explanation.

12. A belief that p may be inconsistent with other beliefs q, r, s, a person holds. But it is important to note that such inconsistency does not mean that a *person* is irrational in holding all four. The importance of this distinction will be developed in the following section.

13. Plantinga (1993b:144–51) also claims that Swinburne's concept of epistemic probability has some debilitating problems. Adjudicating that dispute would go far beyond the bounds of this book; all we need to notice here is that his canons for establishing a rational belief are not uncontested.

14. If Mavrodes is correct at this point, then even if Swinburne had shown that theism has a probability greater than 0.5, he would not have shown that it is irrational not to believe theism or imprudent not to make a religious commitment which includes theistic beliefs.

15. Externalists like Plantinga find "internalism" a thoroughly modern phenomenon which arose (more or less) with Descartes, who attempted to respond to systematic doubt by constructing or discovering internal warrants for claims. This view has been challenged by Zagzebski (1993) among others.

16. Plantinga makes this clear when he claims that the Free Will Defense does not explain why God allows evil in the world, but only that it shows that there might be explanations (see Tilley [1984] and the literature cited there).

17. Plantinga also mounts an argument that skepticism is another possible option for the metaphysical naturalist, but in the interests of (relative) brevity and simplicity, I have omitted it.

18. This modified epistemological externalism should not be confused with the religious externalism formerly described. The earlier account seeks evidence external to religion to show that a religious belief is reasonable.

19. If Alston is correct on this point, and I think he is, he has shown why both some "postliberals" (Lindbeck 1984) and some "experiential-expressivists" (arguably Karl Rahner) are wrong about the place of religious experience in fundamental Christian theology and in philosophy of religion. An "experiential-expressivist" presumption that there is some undifferentiated, prelinguistic or preconceptual experience which an individual has and which underlies the differentiated expressions of that experience misplaces (or neglects) the role background beliefs play in identifying a religious experience. One cannot say that one is having or has had a religious experience unless one has the concepts necessary to make that identification.

A "postliberal" presumption that there is no experience of God unmediated by a cultural symbolic system overemphasizes the role of background beliefs. By accepting the mystics' claims to a *direct, unmediated* experience of the divine, but recognizing belief structures as *ingredients in* rather than *causes of* experience, Alston's work shows a plausible way to account for a tradition's influence on an individual's belief and practice without resorting to contradicting the mystical and commonsense claim to direct experiences.

20. The theologian I had in mind when I wrote these paragraphs is, of course, Matthew Fox. Since this material was written, Fox has left the Roman Catholic Church for the Episcopal Church. On the account here, Fox would have to be described as deciding or discovering that the practices in which he engaged, although nurtured in the Catholic tradition, could no longer be at home in communities where Roman Catholic institutional authorities were part of the overriding mechanism.

21. Of course, a Kierkegaardian or irrationalist might say that this finality is just the point: when we reach the end of reasons, we must choose without them. It may well be true, but it is not clear that we have reached the end of reasons.

22. Like the work of Lorraine Code, the present investigation may sit "uneasily with epistemologists . . . because [its] questions are thought not to be properly epistemological at all, but to belong to ethics, or to the softer fringes of everyday talk about knowledge, rather than to the hard center of serious epistemological analysis. My claim is that if epistemology is indeed about the scope and limits of human knowledge, then it needs to address such questions [of intellectual virtue, social location, etc.] and not just the more formal ones that have been its principal preoccupation" (1994:3). If religious epistemology is also to be about religious knowing, then it needs to address such questions—which is the purpose of the present project.

4

Wisdom in Practice

In the 1956 World Series, Don Larsen of the New York Yankees pitched a perfect game. By all accounts his final pitch in that game was not in the strike zone, but "high and outside." Nonetheless, the umpire called the pitch a strike, so it *was* a strike, and the only perfect game pitched in the history of the World Series was complete.[1] Baseball enthusiasts defend this call. Technically, it was wrong. The umpire missed the call. Either he 'saw' it wrong (and his call was epistemically improper) or he 'called' it wrong (and his call was morally improper). Yet baseball enthusiasts say that it was the right call, because the pitch was close to the strike zone and no batter should not swing at a close pitch in such a crucial situation. In this unusual situation, a technically unwarranted call was nonetheless the wise call for the umpire to make.

Within the game of baseball, and within that particularly momentous game, what appears to an outsider to be a wrong call is the right call. This is not to say that only a fan can understand baseball (or analogously that only a participant can understand a religion). The last chapter claimed that entitlement to hold a belief has no necessary connection with life lived in a particular religious tradition. But this example shows that the connections between proper participation in a practice and the justification of belief and action may be more complex than nonparticipants might imagine. The academic outsider might find that the umpire was not entitled to his belief or to make his call; yet many who love and understand the game know that he did what was proper practice within the game of baseball.

To understand the wisdom of a religious commitment requires understanding what William James called a "full fact": "A conscious field *plus* its object as felt or thought of *plus* the sense of a self to whom the attitude belongs" (James 1902:387). But that self is a social self, formed in a great variety of social spaces. The object is not mere beliefs, but a tradition carried by an institution and communicated by a community. The conscious field is a complex relation between the two. To have a philosophy of religion that recognizes the complexity of religious practices, including believing, finally requires understanding the wisdom of religious commitment. And that demands understanding not merely how to analyze beliefs *in vitro*, but how to understand the many dimensions of religious life, all of which impinge, sometimes obviously, sometimes inchoately, *in vivo*, in the life of the embodied, located, experiencing self.[2]

THE PRESUMPTION OF SUBSTITUTABILITY

Generally, we have so far given philosophers of religion the "presumption of substitutability." Unless they presume that religious beliefs can "stand in for" religious life, they cannot do philosophy of *religion*. They may have been engaging in the modern practice of rational *theology*, defending the rationality of specific beliefs, as Swinburne did. They may have been undertaking rational *apologetics* by showing that the religious person is justified in holding basic beliefs about God because their propositional content (theism) is more warranted by epistemological theory than the view held by their materialist opponents, as Plantinga did. But without making the "presumption of substitutability," what they show by these arguments *in vitro* cannot apply to religions as lived and practiced, religion *in vivo*. Can the examination and justification of the propositional content of religious beliefs apart from religious practices substitute for a philosophical analysis of the "full fact" of religion? Can we give philosophers of religion the "presumption of substitutability"? The obvious answer is no: if analyzing religion cannot be reduced to evaluating the propositional content of religious belief, as I argued in chapter 2, and the "presumption of substitutability" is such a reduction, then it is improper. My answer, however, is a qualified yes: but only within the context of the discourse practice of modern philosophy of religion.

In the introduction and the previous chapters I have alluded to the shape of the discourse of modern philosophy of religion. Basically, its terms are laid down by skeptics. Their purposes seem to be the undermining of the rationality of religious beliefs (or of religious belief generally, if one allows them a "presumption of substitutability"). At the beginning of modern philosophy of religion, some have subjected specific religious beliefs to ridicule. Voltaire's *Candide*, for instance, ridicules the Leibnizian claim that this is the best of all possible worlds.

But Hume's *Dialogues Concerning Natural Religion* is truly the fountain-head. It has determined the shape of the discourse, at least in the English-speaking world, as no other text has. It provides the hidden clue that accounts for the dismissal of religious internalism, the ignoring of religious practices, and the subsequent struggle of Christian philosophers to show religious belief reasonable.

The text is powerful because it is not merely a series of abstract arguments, laid out as a system. Rather it is a script to be enacted, a mimetic narrative of a dialogue among three philosophers, a text that tests its readers and rewards them with considerable satisfaction when they have understood it. The reader is drawn into the text to take the role of the various philosophers, to walk their paths, to understand their arguments, to become what they are. Cleanthes is a philosophical theist, arguing from the nature of the world to the existence of God. He is a paradigm "externalist" in the philosophy of religion. Demea refuses to give any external support for religion; he is labeled as rigidly and inflexibly orthodox and called a "mystic" (almost an "irrational-ist") who refuses to allow any rational argument to provide a foundation for religious faith. In fact, he is really a type of pietist (see Hume 1779:130–31, 193–94) and may be a paradigm "internalist." But these two are inscribed in the text as losers in the argument (despite the final opinion rendered by Pamphilus, the student-auditor of the conversation [228]).

The winner is Philo, a philosophical skeptic, a debater *par excellence* whose wily strategies form the plot of the *Dialogues*. Philo cunningly joins Demea in undermining Cleanthes' philosophical foundations for theism in the first eight parts of the text. He reduces Cleanthes' arguments to absurdity. Philo then stands aside and watches Cleanthes demolish Demea's half-hearted a priori argument for the existence of God in part 9, finally approving Cleanthes' handi-work and adding a few comments of his own. Then he develops a hint from Demea into the full-blown problem of evil in parts 10 and 11 to undermine any attempt to base belief in an all-good, all-powerful God in the course of events:

> And is it possible, Cleanthes, said Philo, that after all these reflections, and infinitely more, which might be suggested, you can still persevere in your anthropomorphism, and assert the moral attributes of the Deity, his justice, benevolence, mercy, and rectitude, to be of the same nature with these virtues in human creatures? His power we allow infinite: Whatever he

wills is executed: But neither man nor any other animal are happy: Therefore he does not will their happiness. His wisdom is infinite: But the course of nature tends not to human or animal felicity: Therefore it is not established for that purpose. Through the whole compass of human knowledge, there are no inferences more certain and infallible than these. In what respects, then, do his benevolence and mercy resemble the benevolence and mercy of men?

Epicurus's Old Questions are yet unanswered. Is he [God] willing to prevent evil, but not able? then is he impotent. Is he able, but not willing? then is he malevolent. Is he both able and willing? whence then is evil? (1779:198)

Here Philo claims that whatever we mean by power, justice, and mercy, etc., when applied to humans has no link whatsoever when we apply those terms to God—a point Antony Flew would raise in a famous and much discussed essay on "Theology and Falsification" some 175 years later. But Demea is appalled by Philo's wild speculations, and withdraws from the conversation. In the 12th and final part, Philo and Cleanthes, finally freed from the "mystic," seem to agree that the only rational religious position is a vague deism.

The *Dialogues* tell the story of "Philo's progress" (see Tilley 1991: 181–84). He tests both Cleanthes' "externalism" and Demea's "internalism." He demolishes the former and dismisses the latter. He comes to prefer Cleanthes' view of the *nature* of true religion as philosophical theism over Demea's view of true religion as pious response or reaction to the world. But such a rational religion cannot have any determinate doctrine or moral content. It is irrelevant to other areas of thought and life. Philo may not speak for Hume directly, but his course in the *Dialogues* sets the pattern for Hume's readers to walk. They are to make progress with the dashing Philo. With him, they learn to reduce externalists to absurdity, to dismiss internalists from any real consideration, to reach his "sober" and "modest" conclusions that the only rational religion is impractical, and to see through the ironic "verdict" impossibly rendered by a student auditor who finds that Cleanthes' principles approach most nearly to the truth. In short, the reader comes to share the real victory with Philo—and thus to take for granted that the only rational religion is theory unrelated to practice.

Many modern academic philosophers of religion make Philo's path their course in universities throughout and even beyond the anglophonic world. One cannot prove the existence of God. Therefore externalist accounts fail to support religious beliefs, and the problem of evil is undefeated, which undermines both internalist and externalist accounts. Therefore, the rational person takes neither path, but remains a mitigated skeptic. The student who follows this course is being led by Hume's clever plot in the *Dialogues* to walk Philo's path.

The conclusion to Hume's *Inquiry Concerning Human Understanding* is often taken as offering in "clear prose" what the *Dialogues* offer in dramatic form. Having endorsed a "mitigated skepticism," he concludes in a famous peroration:

> When we run over libraries, persuaded of these principles, what havoc must we make? If we take in our hand any volume— of divinity or school metaphysics, for instance—let us ask, *Does it contain any abstract reasoning concerning quantity or number?* No. *Does it contain any experimental reasoning concerning matter of fact and existence?* No. Commit it then to the flames, for it can contain nothing but sophistry and illusion (1777:173).

The path of rational progress in philosophy of religion, then, is to become a mitigated skeptic, a vague deist, a debunker of any who would find external support for religious belief, and a despiser of any orthodox internalists who must be so "rigid and inflexible" that they would refuse to play the game to the end.

Given that this plot has been the dominant strand of modern philosophy of religion, certainly in anglophonic academia in this century, what are philosophers who are also religiously committed to do? Are they to walk this path whose end is skepticism? If the discourse of modern philosophy of religion is indeed shaped by this classic text, and philosophers and their students retrace the plot line of "Philo's progress" for themselves, then either religiously committed philosophers need to enter the fray on the skeptics' field and reshape the plot line by showing that the story is not over when the *Dialogues* end or that they need to play on a different field. Not to play on this field is to abandon it to the skeptics, to assist in committing most books of divinity or metaphysics to the flames, and to allow an uncontested victory to Philo and his descendants. The religiously serious philosopher must face this dilemma.

Swinburne and Plantinga do not abandon the field. Against the skeptics, they argue in different ways theists are more rational than atheists. But to play on this field, they have to provide external warrant for religious beliefs. They did not set the terms of the discourse, the rules of the game. They accept the challenge to provide an externalist "foundation" for religious belief. For the purposes of playing the "game," their goal must be the examination and justification of religious beliefs without regard to religious practices. Such an examination must substitute in this context for a philosophical analysis of the "full fact" of religion. If the plot is to be given a new twist, these voices must be heard within the discourse.

This discourse practice has been accepted as legitimate in the academy. In this context, we must give philosophers of religion, both friends and enemies of religion, the "presumption of substitutability." For without it, religiously committed philosophers must walk with Demea out of the conversation. The practical result of total withdrawal is making their insights and arguments irrelevant. Therefore, my qualified yes to the "presumption of substitutability": the qualification is the legitimacy of the discourse practice. If there is only one game in town and if one cannot reach one's goal without playing it, then it is obviously wise to play the game and accept the initial conditions even if the deck is stacked against one.

But is the discourse practice legitimate? Or is it in need not only of a fourth voice, but of extensive reform? Can the discourse be reshaped from a skeptical academic pattern into a more practical one? The pattern of the last chapter suggests it can reshaped, that the plot can be rewritten. Swinburne plays the game as given. He argues for the rationality of theism on rational grounds available to any who would enter the arena of argument. Plantinga reshapes the practice in an important way by introducing his naturalized approach (influenced by Thomas Reid). In doing this, he shifts the burden of proof off the religious believer's shoulders. It is important to see what this shift is. In terms drawn from his earlier work, we can see how he makes this shift.

One can describe two sorts of beliefs in a person's set of beliefs: basic and nonbasic.[3] Descriptively, basic beliefs are not based on other beliefs; nonbasic beliefs are derived from or based on other beliefs. Normatively, one's beliefs can be proper or improper.

Proper basic beliefs are those beliefs which one is warranted in holding on grounds other than one's other beliefs. For example, experience, testimony, and memory may be such grounds, and unless we have reason to doubt them, we are warranted in relying on these sources of beliefs. For instance, we doubt someone's testimony when we come to know that he or she is a habitual liar. But unless such defeating conditions obtain, our belief in that testimony is warranted.

Proper derived beliefs are those beliefs which one is warranted in holding on the basis of other beliefs. Inference and generalization etc., may be such grounds. For instance, when we open a door and walk through it, we expect to find a floor on the other side; most times we do, and unless some special defeating condition obtains, such as a sign reading "stairs" on the door or exploring a building with Indiana Jones, we ordinarily and properly expect a floor on the other side of a door when we walk through it. Of course it is possible that it was ripped away while we weren't looking (it is fun to watch students leave class after working through this material in a philosophy class), but we are warranted in our (usually inchoate) belief that there is a floor outside the door on the basis of a generalization from our past experience. It is a properly derived belief.

Improper basic beliefs are basic beliefs which one holds and that one is not warranted in holding. They were formed when defeating conditions obtained. For example, examining a piece of paper in bright yellow light may be a condition under which we cannot properly form a belief that the paper is yellow because it might easily be white or beige. The yellow light is one example of a defeating condition. If we come to see that defeating conditions obtain, we should drop the belief itself because its warrant was "defeated" by those conditions.

Improper nonbasic beliefs are those which one holds on the basis of other beliefs which are either warranted only by improper basic beliefs or not properly warranted by the process or method which one employed to reach them from one's basic beliefs. Errors in logic, miscalculations, improper use of probabilities, or using an inappropriate method to derive such beliefs would be defeating conditions. If, from testimony, I believe that most Americans are overweight, and I learn that Marian is an American, and I infer that Marian is certainly overweight, I have stretched probability beyond the breaking point. My belief would be improper, unwarranted.

But is it possible that belief in God can be properly basic for theists? Yes. In many cases it can easily be seen to be basic as it arises out of their experiences and the religious education that they receive. No philosopher has developed (or probably could develop) a credible criterion for proper basicality that could show that such beliefs were improper. Plantinga has argued that in certain conditions belief in God may be, even for mature theists, an exemplary proper basic belief. Plantinga writes:

> There are therefore many conditions and circumstances that call
> forth belief in God: guilt, gratitude, danger, a sense of God's
> presence, a sense that he speaks, perception of various parts of
> the universe. A complete job would explore the phenomenology
> of all these conditions and of more besides. This is a large and
> important topic; but here I can only point to the existence of
> these conditions (Plantinga 1983:81).

However, Plantinga does not analyze the ways in which communities
of discourse shape the beliefs we take to be basic. He acknowledged
this when he noted that he had not done a "complete job" of exploring
the conditions and circumstances which produce basic religious beliefs. Rather, he takes it for granted that belief in God is properly
basic because such belief is generated by our cognitive faculties functioning as they were designed to function in an appropriate—a God-
given—environment. He is warranted in taking it for granted because
that is just what we do. We take it for granted that our beliefs are
proper unless we are shown that defeating conditions occur, that is,
unless we have good reason to doubt that they are warranted. The
argument for the superiority of theism recounted in chapter 3 shows
why theists are clearly within their cognitive rights to find such a belief
properly basic, undefeated by the attempts of atheists and agnostics
to undermine it, and thus clearly warranted. Given the arguments
recounted in chapter 3, some theists have good reason not only not
to doubt the warrant for their beliefs, but also to believe that their
basic belief in God, whether generated by experience, testimony, or
other methods is proper.

Whether the discourse dominated by the *Dialogues* can be reshaped into a truly practical pattern that attends to the conditions
and circumstances that call forth religious belief remains to be seen.
Arguments like Swinburne's and Plantinga's, even if successful, do
not show the wisdom of any particular religious commitment; they
do, however, defend (at least some) religious commitments in general
from attack and shift the burden of proof to the atheist.

Note, however, that even given the "presumption of substitutability," this approach does not resolve the practical problem of finding
a wise religious commitment, for many traditions take belief in God
as central and distinctive. If Plantinga's arguments support any one
of them (and I think they do, at least "academically"), they support
all of them. But we can't be committed to all of them. Jews, Muslims,
Christians of various stripes, some theistic Hindus, and perhaps others could make arguments practically identical to Plantinga's. Even if

theism is in a position epistemically superior to atheism, many of the various theists (and, by extension, the theisms that can be abstracted from their religious beliefs) are on an epistemic par.

Clearly, if we are to go beyond this level of academic generality, we need to explore a practical approach which does not participate in the mainstream philosophical tradition. Human beings are not minds, not rational machines. We are embodied social selves who live in multiple social locations, including religious or quasi-religious ones. The formal religious spaces we inhabit are constituted by traditions carried by institutions and embodied in communities. To go forward in philosophy of religion, we need to abandon the Humean pattern of academic disputation and attend to the practices people undertake religiously, practices like attending Mass and taking holy water, for these practices, along with others, generate religious beliefs for the embodied people who participate in them. We must also attend to the communal, institutional, and traditional contexts in which people develop beliefs. The final epistemic issue, then, is practical. The question is not one of having warranted theoretical "knowledge that," but practical wisdom, prudence or *phronesis*, to know how to make a wise religious commitment (compare Zagzebski: 1993; Code 1994).

But "prudence" is not a univocal term and cannot be simply equated with probability judgments or judgments about the course of action that will be in one's (narrowly conceived) self-interest. Nor can prudence be equated with rule-following behavior, for it is the practice of applying rules and of understanding which rules apply or don't apply in a situation. Prudence, or practical wisdom, as "know how," involves more than probability and self-interest. The question is what does practical wisdom or prudence look like?

THE PRACTICE OF WISDOM

How does a person put wisdom into practice? What is the ability to put intellect into action and to draw theory from practice? Even to begin to answer such questions, we must look at specific contexts, for wisdom is not a principle to be defended by argument, but a virtue to be displayed through narrative. This answer entails a certain level of vagueness (Zagzebski 1993:215–16), but that is unavoidable in showing a virtue.

Philosophers sometimes equate or closely connect practical wisdom with probability calculations. But consider the proposition that a score will occur on a specific play in an American college football game. Scores occur on few plays, but there is some probability that a score by one team or the other will result from any play. The probability varies with the abilities of the players and coaches, the teams' positions on the field, the type of play being run, and luck. Some plays, for example, a field goal attempted by a good kicker on a fourth-down-and-goal-to-go with the line of scrimmage inside the ten yard line, have a probability approaching one (100 percent) of scoring three points for the offensive team and a probability approaching 0 (0 percent) of scoring six points for either team. Other plays, for example, a pass in the same situation, have a significantly lower probability of scoring for the offense (although they would, if successful, score more points), and a significantly higher, but still very small, probability of scoring six points for the defense.

Given that a coach knows the probabilities, is the coach prudent to call for a field goal attempt in the situation described, knowing that the probability of a "positive result" on the field goal is far higher than the probability of a "positive result" on a pass play? Is this the prudent choice? We can't say. We don't have enough information about the conditions that obtain. The answer will depend on a whole host of factors (e.g., the score and the time left in the game) that go far beyond the probabilities of scoring. Philosopher George Mavrodes has claimed that "to the extent that prudent action can be assimilated to betting, it seems to be a proper function of estimates of probability, not of strength of belief" (Mavrodes 1982:67). But that analysis is incomplete. Other circumstances affect the issue. Pure probabilities cannot determine how a coach should act in every circumstance. If the score is ten to seven, with a few seconds left in the game, the coach's action may properly be a function of his strong beliefs about the long-term difference for the team between a win and a tie, rather than the probability of scoring on a specific play.

The probability of scoring six points on a pass may be significantly lower than scoring three points on a field goal, but if the coach strongly believes that a tie is not in the long-term interests of the team, the coach may reasonably choose a course less probable to produce a score. And the coach's belief that it is better to attempt to score a touchdown in those circumstances and acting on it may be controversial. Yet the controversy arises not because his belief is irrational, for it is not irrational to act to win games rather than to avoid losing them, but because such action may be imprudent. It is to only a limited extent that prudent action seems to be a function of probability estimates.

In the coach's situation, what could make calling a play less probable to score than another a prudent action? The obvious answer is that the coach's beliefs about winning and losing a specific game, and about what action is in the long-term interest of the team make the action he chooses seem prudent to him. But as Mavrodes's argument suggests, a prudent person does not have to believe either that a proposition is true or that it has a probability greater than 0.5 to act on it in certain situations. Other beliefs and values that the coach holds may well make the choice of an action with less probability of success over another action with a greater probability of success a prudent choice.

The question remains, however, whether the coach's action *is* prudent. Monday-morning quarterbacks often raise this question. Really controversial choices can provoke almost as much discussion as the umpire's call in Larson's perfect baseball game. Arguments go on because we cannot put prudence on a scale quite so neatly as Swinburne put rationality on a scale.[4] Prudence is not algorithmic. One might program a very complex computer to be "rational" in Swinburne's sense of the term. But prudential choice and prudential action is not programmable. One might say that prudential choice cannot follow a program, but is the ability to choose the best program to follow in a given situation. It is the skill of understanding which rules apply to a given case, an aptitude for choosing the right tools to use for the job at hand. It is the capacity for figuring out which practices are best to follow. Prudence is not "purely subjective" or just a matter of opinion. It is a virtue to be developed. Wisdom cannot be calculated, but neither is it arbitrary. It can only be displayed—and, one hopes, emulated.

Nonetheless, one can discriminate among simpler and more complex exercises of wisdom. One can discern increasing difficulty and richness in prudential choices and actions. As Swinburne claimed that rationality was not a univocal term, so wisdom is not univocal. But as wisdom becomes more complex, more complex narratives are needed to discern wise from unwise choices. By borrowing from Swinburne's pattern, I do not mean to imply that there are "levels" of wisdom, but to indicate that there are easier and harder kinds of issues for a prudent person to resolve.

A prudent$_1$ action is one that is consistent with an agent's beliefs. An action that is inconsistent with an agent's beliefs is imprudent$_1$. Consider the football coach introduced above. If the coach believes that the probability of a pass play scoring is zero, and calls for a pass when a score is necessary, the coach performs an imprudent action. To look for a result that one believes cannot occur is absurd. Thus, such an action fails to be prudent in the most fundamental way. However, to call for a pass play in a situation in which a score is necessary to win, even if the probability of the play scoring is negligible, is *not* necessarily an imprudent choice. Fans of quarterbacks Fran Tarkenton and Doug Flutie will surely recall successful "Hail Mary" passes thrown in desperation from beyond the fifty yard line. That an action has only a negligible chance of success is neither a necessary nor a sufficient condition of labeling an action "imprudent." If among the choices facing one, all but one are certain to yield failure to reach one's goal, then even if that one possibility is highly improbable, it is "the only game in town," and it is obviously wise to choose it—a prudential judgment appropriate not only for football coaches, but for academic philosophers of religion.

A prudent$_2$ action is one that follows properly from an agent's assumptions. An action reached by using faulty warrants is imprudent$_2$. For instance, consider the difference between attempting a long field goal and attempting to score a touchdown on a long pass when a field goal will tie the score, but a touchdown will win the game. If a coach knows that one play has a high probability of success and the other a low probability of equal success (e.g., either a win or a tie in this game will enable the team to make the playoffs), and chooses the low probability play on a lark, the coach's action is based on faulty warrants, and is imprudent. Although it may not be possible to calculate the probabilities precisely, part of the skill a coach learns is to estimate them and to evaluate their relevance on the spot—to put intellect into action. Notice that the successful completion of a play is neither a necessary nor a sufficient condition for calling the choice of the play prudent; what tells here is the way the coach assesses the probabilities.

In situations like this, Mavrodes's dictum about probability seems most likely to apply. Assumptions about the probabilities of success are sufficient to call a choice in line with the probabilities prudent. What would make a choice apparently out of line with the probabilities and nonetheless prudent would be "defeating conditions." For instance, a muddy field may make all the usual calculations of probabilities unreliable. Or in more complex cases, "special circumstances" may obtain in which it is prudent to choose against the probabilities. For instance, football teams have tendencies. In each type of situation, there is a statistical probability of the offensive team running a specific type of play because it is usually successful for them (say, a twelve yard pass to one of three receivers on third down and ten yards to go). Since the coach of the team on defense knows it, the defensive team is usually set to defend against the pass play. In light of this, the offensive coach may then decide to run a play with a lower probability of succeeding (say a running play like a "draw play" for the fullback) to "cross up" the defense. In such conditions and circumstances, it may well be prudent to choose against the probabilities. Again, success or failure on a specific choice is not clearly relevant to the wisdom of the choice.

It seems that persons believe they are acting prudently when their acts seem prudent$_1$ and prudent$_2$. Of course, after the fact, an agent may come to realize that a certain act was imprudent. Perhaps disastrous consequences of the action will make the agent reevaluate the wisdom of performing it. Perhaps the realization that one avoided the disastrous consequences of an imprudent act only by luck, e.g., driving drunk yet arriving safely at one's destination, will get the agent to rethink the warrants. Good or bad consequences of an action may be symptoms of, but not conditions for, an act to be right or wrong.[5] But the possibility of reconsidering the prudence of what once seemed a prudent act raises the issue of even more complex choices, of prudence$_3$.

A prudent$_3$ act is one that is prudent$_{1,2}$ and whose assumptions and warrants have been checked to a degree adequate for that agent. Relevant considerations include the (a) probability or propriety of the agent's assumptions; (b) warrants the agent uses in inferring the right act; (c) proper delineation of goal of the action; (d) importance of the action given the expectation that any investigation undertaken will be useful and given the time and energy the agent has available for investigation. An imprudent$_3$ act is one for which the agent has failed to check the assumptions, inferential warrants, and goals properly.

Many discussions of practical wisdom center on prudence$_3$ and involve questions typically discussed as the "ethics of belief."[6] Here the notions of duty to understand properly come into play, for the ability to reflect, rather than the routine exercise of habit, is the key to prudence$_3$. Prudence$_3$ is prudent action that goes beyond probability calculations or practical inferences in significant ways.

(a) A prudent$_3$ act requires appropriate checking of the agent's factual assumptions or probability beliefs, or both. An act is imprudent₃ if it is based on *culpably* erroneous assumptions. For instance, if a football coach ignores or is oblivious to the fact that the kicker has just pulled a groin muscle, and calls for a long field goal on the probabilities established when the kicker was healthy, the coach's action is imprudent. It is the responsibility of the coach to know the condition of the players and how it affects the play. Perhaps a breakdown of communication led to the coach having a false belief. No one told him that the kicker was injured. In some circumstances, it may be impossible to say who was at fault; the breakdown may have been caused by the failure of the head coach, assistant, trainer, or player. Nonetheless, this situation is an example of one in which an agent bases an act on a false assumption that the agent should have known was false. This false assumption renders the act imprudent.

The responsibility for checking an assumption on which an act is based is a "role-specific" responsibility. Agents' moral responsibilities vary with regard to their roles.[7] This concept has been elucidated by Van A. Harvey's reflections on the strengths and weaknesses of W. K. Clifford's classic essay, "The Ethics of Belief."

Clifford used the example of a shipowner who sends his old, worn-out ship to sea, despite the fact that he had good reason to doubt its seaworthiness. The shipowner simply stifled those doubts. If the ship then sank with all hands, the shipowner would be "guilty of the death of those men . . . because he had no right to believe on such evidence as was before him" (Clifford 1877:19). He had no right to believe because he fails, Clifford argues, in his duty as a human being to believe only upon adequate evidence. Even if the ship made port, and the passengers and crew did not suffer for his choice, he would still be guilty, according to Clifford. He believed, perhaps sincerely by the time the ship weighed anchor, that the ship was seaworthy. But sincerity is not adequate evidence and stifling doubts not a proper method of belief development.

Harvey (1979) has pointed out that such duties are not general human duties, but role-specific ones. The owner of the ship, but not a passenger in it (or a cabin attendant working on it), is obliged to check the assumption that the ship was seaworthy before it sailed loaded with passengers just because the owner has the role of owner. Today it is the pilot of an airliner who has the role-specific responsibility of making a preflight walkaround check. The management has the responsibility of hiring only qualified pilots and ensuring that they know their jobs, but they do not have the responsibility to perform the preflight check. The responsibility of allowing a ship loaded with passengers and cargo to sail or an airliner to leave the gate for takeoff would not apply to "anyone," but is specific to the role of shipowner or pilot. These role-specific responsibilities tie each of them to their "wider duty to the culture and to the safety of its citizens. One fulfills this wider duty by being responsible for one's narrower station and its duties" (Harvey 1979:198).

People in other roles or stations do not have the same responsibility to check the vessel's seaworthiness, although they have other duties that contribute to a successful voyage. A shipowner does not have the responsibility to know whether pirates had just been spotted near the ship's destination across the sea. To protect the vessel from pirates is the navy's duty. The pilot does not have the responsibility for air traffic control: that is the controller's duty.

On this analysis, a prudent$_3$ act would be done in accord with the usual standards by which people in that role or undertaking normally act. Football fans making a friendly wager on whether a field goal will be made, naturally assume that a kicker running on to the field is healthy. Bets are normally not imprudent if such bettors assume the kicker to be healthy and if the probabilities of his success are normal. They are not in a role that normally requires checking the health of the kicker. Nor are the other players, the opposing teams, or anyone not responsible for making the play selection or informing the person who is responsible for play selection.

The notion of "role-specificity" introduces a necessarily social component to the analysis of practical wisdom. Whether we choose our roles or are "assigned to" them by the fates, the gods, or the circumstances in which we find ourselves, the roles themselves are social constructs. Although the narratives exemplifying prudence$_1$ and prudence$_2$ rely on concrete situations in which the actors are in certain roles, the conditions for prudence$_1$ and prudence$_2$ are not role-specific, but belief-specific. A person is prudent$_1$ if her actions do not go against her beliefs and prudent$_2$ if her actions follow from her beliefs. Prudence$_1$ is weakly tied to an agent's warranted beliefs and prudence$_2$ is more strongly tied to an agent's warranted beliefs. In contrast prudence$_3$ involves role-specific duties. Perhaps it is impossible to exemplify prudence without reference to social roles, socially established practice, and social contexts because actions are always performed in contexts and because we are embodied and find ourselves necessarily in (or more rarely, creating) roles. It might seem arbitrary to introduce role-specificity only at this level of complexity. However, in common exercises of prudence, the distinctive questions about role-specific duties do not even arise if an act fails to be prudent₁ and prudent₂.

(b) A prudent₃ action requires appropriate warrant, sufficiently checked by the agent. An act is imprudent₃ if the inferences about the means to reach the goal were inappropriate. If a basketball coach has miscalculated the probabilities of successful inbounding of a ball on an "inbound play," her warrant is flawed. Perhaps it is flawed by insufficient care about an opposing player's strength or leaping ability or speed—who then breaks up the play and steals the ball. Perhaps the coach forgets that she has only one play available from a certain formation and has used it twice earlier in the game—and the opponents steal the ball because they anticipate where the ball will be thrown. But the flawed warrant renders the coach's act imprudent.

Similarly, if the probabilities of equal success are clearly different for different possible actions, then hunches, guesses, and wishful thinking are examples of inappropriate guides for a coach's choice. However, calling a play with a marginally lower probability or probability range on the basis of a "hunch" may be prudent. Or a coach may choose to call a play for which the opposing team will be unprepared because of its improbability in the situation, but which, if attempted, may be a success. In these situations where probabilities of success can only be estimated very roughly and where vastly different outcomes are possible, it seems neither necessary nor sufficient for an act to be imprudent if the coach bases it on a hunch. A coach may talk of the "feel of the game" and sportscasters of "momentum" as providing warrants for a coach's play calling. Coaches may well find themselves in a situation that cannot be decided on grounds of probability or rationality; consequently, they may have to rely on luck, chance, or "intuition" to warrant their acts. In sum, prudent inferential warrants are not only role-specific, but also situation specific. Thus, the communal and institutional constructs which shape our various social locations are relevant to understanding and evaluating prudence.

The question is the sufficiency of the checking. The evil demon of skepticism threatens to raise its ugly head here. When is checking enough checking? Isn't it possible that despite all our investigations our choices might be imprudent? But in practice, checking necessarily has its limits. And in practices, appropriate checks are defined. For instance, the preflight walkaround by the pilot is an "eyeball" check.

Pilots ordinarily use flashlights to check places in the shadows, but do not carry micrometers to measure the thickness of the airplane's skin or tread depth on tires. If something doesn't look right, the pilot has to pursue the investigation to find out whether it is safe to fly.

The question of checking is a practical issue, with benchmarks established in institutional and communal contexts. Perhaps the best example is diagnosis in medicine. An obstetrician who is surprised at delivery when two babies are born, rather than the expected one, has clearly failed to do enough checking, and the failure to check sufficiently is malpractice, even if no serious harm is done to the family.

Prudent medical practice, however, varies from situation to situation. Consider joint injuries. An emergency physician who fails to x-ray an injured knee upon which a patient cannot put weight is not checking appropriately. An x-ray, a clinical history, and physical exam are necessary. However, the use of magnetic resonance imaging for joint injuries is currently rarely indicated. It is expensive and time consuming. Only in specific cases can it yield information that would significantly change the treatment of an injury. A physician who uses magnetic resonance imaging routinely is checking too much. A physician who fails to prescribe regular mammograms for female patients over fifty fails to check enough. We know this because the physician fails to come up to the normal standards that the medical community has come to accept.

Prudent practice also varies from place to place. In urban locations where highly developed medical institutions have the latest in equipment and techniques abundantly available, proper diagnosis may involve using them regularly. In a rural practice, where such equipment and techniques are not readily available, it may be good practice to "make do" without them as a rule, but to transport certain patients to a city in special circumstances. The social location and the institutional location of the practitioner can bring different standards of practice into play.

Standards for checking are internal to the practice, but external to the individual practitioner. The goal of proper investigation is to make prudent action possible, not to warrant knowing indefeasibly. An individual may change the standards of the practice, but standards of good practice remain external to the individual. And checking is practice-specific, location-specific, and role-specific. Part of the wise physician's, the wise pilot's, the wise coach's, and the wise shipowner's skill is to know how much standard practice requires one to investigate the situation of one's patient, one's airplane, one's game plan, or one's ship—and when to deviate from standard practice.

Occasionally, despite appropriate checking, agents will make errors. This contingency does not, however, count against the theory of practical wisdom. It is not possible to specify algorithmically what rules apply in which circumstances. That choice has to be left to the agent. People will make mistakes even if they are doing what the epistemologist, whether theoretical or practical, would find proper. The possibility of error is part of the human condition, and an unavoidable fact.

(c) Acts may be imprudent$_3$ if the desired ends are not delineated clearly enough given the situation. For instance, consider B. F. Pierce, M.D., of "MASH 4077," who has spent long hours in the surgical theater trying to patch up soldiers wounded in a battle to take a worthless hill. He listens to the soldiers complain of the muleheadedness of their commander, Colonel Lacy, who wants to take the hill even though his company has sustained terrible losses in previous sorties. He hears the colonel contriving to sidestep orders forbidding him to try to take the hill again. In an effort to save the company's surviving soldiers from useless carnage, Pierce violates his Hippocratic oath. He induces a bellyache in the colonel, examines him, "diagnoses" appendicitis, and removes the colonel's healthy appendix in order to force headquarters to send another, less irrational, officer to take command of the unit while Lacy recuperates from his "life-saving" surgery.

In the television episode, Pierce seems to be placed in the classic moral dilemma of doing evil to achieve good: either he can do the conventionally unethical act of performing useless surgery on the colonel, thus serving a morally praiseworthy end—for the surgery would indeed be life-saving, but for the company, not the colonel— or he can act in accordance with the rules and not do the surgery, thus allowing the colonel to command the carnage to continue. The probability of significant injury to the colonel is negligible and the probability of preventing foolish sacrifice of soldiers' lives seems high. The episode is written so that the audience is led to root for Hawkeye Pierce as he chooses and executes the conventionally immoral act. Dr. Pierce *seems* to be stepping up to a higher level of morality, that is, to be cutting through convention into a paradoxically creative moral choice.

As the episode continues, however, so does the carnage of the Korean War. The battles rage on, and Pierce is recalled to the operating room to save more soldiers' lives. In a conversation with his pal, Dr. B. J. Honeycutt, Pierce comes to see that the action in violation of his Hippocratic Oath was truly imprudent. What made it imprudent was neither Pierce's intentions, nor his violation of the rules of conventional morality and role-specific duties, nor his use of a consequentialist calculus in his moral reasoning, nor even the danger in which he placed the colonel. The story plays so that the viewer would have seen the prudence of Pierce's act if it could have achieved its aim. What clearly made it imprudent was that Hawkeye's bogus surgery could not succeed in reaching his goal. He aimed to stop the slaughter. He removed one colonel. But, as Honeycutt points out, Pierce misidentified the scope of the problem. The problem was not one colonel's lack of judgment, but the whole insanity of the war. Hawkeye couldn't see that disabling one person from performing acts that maimed people did nothing to resolve the socially evil context in which and only in which maiming and slaughter not only can be performed, but must be performed repeatedly.

Sidelining one participant, as much a victim of the war as others, could not contribute anything to solving the real problem. To use theological language, Pierce's idea that removing Lacy would contribute to ending the slaughter was based on conflating personal sin with communal or institutional evil. Hawkeye presumed that if he sidelined the commander, he would remove the evil the commander was doing and the carnage his men were suffering. But the commander was not the only one responsible for the killing and maiming. The only way to stop the carnage was to end the war. And if one chose to stop the war by removing the whole command structure, to complete that task would take another war, a rather bloody revolution—a depressingly self-defeating tactic. In another institutional context, removing a bad leader from a leadership position might "work." But given Pierce's situation and the institutional structures involved, the act could not achieve its goal.[8]

Pierce's process of inference, though probably prudent$_2$, was not prudent$_3$ because he did not delineate the goal of his act sufficiently to evaluate the utility of the means at his disposal as a surgeon in the army. The process of inference is seriously flawed because he misidentifies the problems the actions are designed to solve: the problems are social problems beyond resolution by this specific agent in this role and this situation with the means available to him. It is not one of those rare cases in which an individual or small group is positioned unilaterally to change the pattern of a practice or to resolve a social problem singlehandedly.[9] Hawkeye fails to act in a prudent manner because he failed to be clear about its relationship to his goals.

(d) Other considerations also apply to an act being prudent$_3$. These are the importance of the action, the expectation that any investigation undertaken will be useful, and the time and energy the agent has available for investigation.

For instance, fans betting a beer on the outcome of a game can presumably afford either to lose or win the wager. Nothing important rides on the outcome of their bet. However, change the situation to one in which a gambler is betting the rent money, and the importance of the bet is radically altered. Gamblers betting the rent money must do a lot more checking on their assumptions than if they were betting a beer. In brief, the more momentous the choice, the more investigation it deserves. While the proper amount of investigation is not quantifiable, big gamblers who spend no time checking their varying assumptions and probabilities will quickly lose enough to have to give up gambling—unless, of course, they are extremely lucky. But if they are "extremely lucky," they cannot be performing prudent acts, given the situation.

The usefulness of investigation, and the energy and time available for investigation and deliberation, may also determine whether an action is wise. A person may be forced to act before a deadline. The football fans, presuming they knew the conditions and the kicker's abilities, could not make a useful investigation between third and fourth downs. If acting is unavoidable and the deadline inescapable, a little-investigated choice may nonetheless be prudent. In a case in which time and energy for deliberation are not available, like those in which the probabilities for equal success of alternative actions are about the same, hunches may warrant a prudent act.

In sum, a prudent$_3$ act is one in which the agent has checked the assumptions and warrants for an action properly, and clearly delineated the goal of the proposed action, given the agent's role and other constraints. Human agents are necessarily embodied agents acting in specific social locations, limited by their own abilities, guided by the standards of the practice they undertake, and shaped by the roles they have as well as by other conditions.

A prudent$_4$ agent is one who performs prudent$_3$ acts in conformity with the standards of excellence appropriate to the agent's stations, positions, or roles. An agent is imprudent$_4$ if the agent fails, consciously or not, to act in conformity to the agent's roles. In effect, we have now reached the complexity of a prudent *person*, for prudent *people* are those who habitually check the assumptions on which their actions are based to an extent proportionate to their role-specific responsibilities. We can no longer talk of acts or patterns of practice that display or embody practical wisdom. For if prudence is a virtue, it is most fully displayed by persons, not acts.

This way of displaying a prudent agent accounts for the fact that some people appear prudent *simpliciter* while others seem prudent in some fields yet imprudent in others. Physicians who typically act prudently in treating their patients may be imprudent in their sexual practice. A brilliant music-dramatist may pen obscene anti-Semitisms. A conscientious shipowner may beat her children unmercifully. The pious priest and famous spiritual director may drive an automobile so rashly that anyone else getting in the car should be automatically eligible for the last rites. Some people have developed the ability habitually to act prudently only in some roles; others have developed that ability in most or all of their social roles. The former we may construe as prudent physicians, priests, coaches, but the latter we can construe as prudent people.[10] This account also explains why people stumble over the conundrum of calling someone a "good" Nazi and yet not a "good" person: the former considers only one role a person plays, while the latter considers the expectations of the panoply of social roles a person plays and is expected to play. A fully prudent person, then, is one who displays a pattern of wise action in all one's roles and situations.

A prudent person also seeks to avoid having conflicting "role-specific responsibilities." Conflicts can be caused by a person having incompatible roles. In one sense, the conflict is obvious—as some classic oxymorons show: for example Buddhist butcher, Baptist bootlegger, Confucian rebel, etc. A prudent Theravadin Buddhist could not be a butcher, nor a prudent Baptist a bootleggger.

For some people, conflicts in responsibilities are unavoidable. Given the social context, single working parents know that conflicts in responsibilities to one's children and one's job will arise. These conflicts produce substantial stress for many simply because they cannot fulfill all of their role-specific responsibilities. It may not be imprudent to hold incompatible roles, at least for a time, given that the incommensurable goods they make possible are highly desirable or given that one could not achieve one sort of good, such as providing the basic necessities of one's children, if one gave up the role that made those goods possible, such as employment to produce the needed income. But it would be imprudent to choose freely to add a role with responsibilities in conflict with a role one already has and wants to keep.

Of course, as we saw in chapter 1 in the example from Lorraine Code (1991), our society places people in situations in which they have insoluble role conflicts. The welfare mother who cannot follow the rules of the system because the system presumes she can do what she must in a timely manner and also forbids her from having the resources necessary (e.g., a car) to have enough time to fulfill her responsibilities is a prime example. It is possible that our social structures are such that few, if any, can become persons who are practically wise in all the roles they must assume. Clearly, our social structures "disempower" many; but it is also true that they can prohibit people who know how to carry out one practice well from carrying that skill into another area of their lives.

Since many practices in which we engage are role- or status-specific, another aspect of prudence$_4$ is the wisdom of participating in a particular practice. Here Alston's arguments as presented in chapter 3 are useful. Obviously, if there are universal and unavoidable human practices, such as perceptual practices, the question of participating in them cannot arise.[11] Such practices are basic to other practices. But even perception is a practice, with its exemplary Sherlocks and its bumbling Watsons. In this sense basic social skills are practices we learn. Even if we have a natural capacity to engage in basic practices, we must develop those capacities practically, by working at developing them.

However, many of the practices in which we engage, especially those that are socially constituted, are also practices that can be tacitly or explicitly chosen. In such cases, the question of the wisdom of participation in those practices can arise. Is it prudent for a person to participate in those practices?

For those practices which we implicitly choose, or which are practically unavoidable given our circumstances, such as being a patriotic American, Canadian, or French citizen, a version of Alston's "conservative" advice seems right: absent external reasons for supposing that one of the competing practices is better than my own, the only prudent course for me is to sit tight with the practice of which I am a master and which serves me so well in guiding my activity in the world (compare Alston 1991:274). In the absence of good reasons to move, "stay home," is good advice.

However, if one comes to see that there may well be external reasons to doubt one's practice or to think that another practice may be superior, or if one comes to see that one's practice is degraded, one *ipso facto* acquires the option (and, perhaps, the duty) to choose among practices. For example, in the 1960s many Americans believed that standard pattern of the practice of patriotism was degraded by their involvement in the Vietnam War. Some left the United States for Canada or Sweden in order to avoid participation in the standard patriotic practice of going to war at the command of the government. Others remained at home and resisted the draft, protested the war, and engaged in other forms of civil disobedience. Some of these even claimed to be "*true* patriots," especially when confronted with sloganeering alleging their lack of patriotism (e.g., "America: Love It or Leave It"). Others remained and fought in the war, some opposing the war effort when they could, others supporting it wholeheartedly as an expression of patriotism. These painful divisions show what happens when one comes to question a practice in which one has been taught to engage and to which one has given tacit consent. At such times, whether by questions arising from within or without the practice, one needs to consider the wisdom of participating in the practice. And this consideration requires an exercise in prudential$_4$ judgment, for the issue is not consistency with beliefs or roles, as in prudential$_{1-3}$ judgments, but the question of the role itself and of the practices that constitute patriotism. That even today Americans debate which of their responses was best with regard to the Vietnam war suggests that the issue is not settled, that we don't know or can't establish a consensus over which was the prudent$_4$ path. When practices are in conflict, and we are not fully committed to one of them (whether our commitment itself is undermined or whether circumstances seem to be forcing us to choose among practices) we must investigate the question of whether a prudent person should participate in them.

As Swinburne found that a rational$_4$ belief is a rational$_3$ belief held by a generally reasonable person, so here we claim that a prudent$_4$

agent is one who performs prudent$_3$ acts in conformity with the standards appropriate to her or his various stations, positions, or roles; who does not take up roles with conflicting duties; and who, when appropriate, investigates the practices in which she or he is engaged.

If the parallel to Swinburne's rationality calculus held, then a prudent$_5$ agent would be one who is prudent$_4$, and who conforms to the "really adequate" prudential standards. Agents would be imprudent$_5$ if their acts were role-specifically prudent$_3$ and they were a generally prudent$_4$ agents, but they now fail to conform to objective standards of prudence. But here we run into a stone wall: the whole point of practical wisdom is that it is not universal, but particular. One exercises wisdom in particular situations. There are, of course, similarities between situations, and patterns of wise practice. But a universal pattern would have to be so general or abstract that putting it into practice in every situation would be of little relevance in discerning the relevant particulars and taking proper action. Practical wisdom cannot be displayed universally because that would require a universal narrative. Even if such a story could be told, it would take the mind of God to understand it.

At this point someone might object that this entails the denial of objective moral standards, for practical wisdom is a "bridge virtue" that incorporates elements of both intellectual and moral virtue. However, the quest for an objective morality runs into quicksand. A concept of what is a "really adequate" objective morality seems as essentially contested as Swinburne's claim to have found the "really adequate" rationale for ultimate claims. Beyond debates over deontological warrants, various forms of consequentialist warrants, and natural law warrants, it is not at all clear that choice is the key to morality: some might follow Murdoch (1970) and claim vision is key, while others might follow MacIntyre (1984) and find a virtue ethic to be the correct moral approach. Finally, noncognitivists, radical emotivists, and some poststructuralist theorists argue that a rational morality is not possible. How are we to pick our way out of this morass of essentially contested claims? Even if there is a true solution, it is certainly not universally recognized. Thus, if a prudent$_5$ agent is a prudent$_4$ agent who conforms to an objective standard of morality, then we cannot recognize agents as prudent$_5$ for the objective standard of morality by which we would attempt to recognize them is essentially contested.[12]

The first step in finding a way around the wall without falling into the swamp of relativism is to recognize a crucial social fact. We live in a world in which we cannot avoid internalizing and participating in practices which make conflicting demands on us. The fact that many, perhaps all, cannot become truly prudent$_4$ agents ought to wake us to the fact that the traditions, communities, and institutions which constitute our roles and ourselves can and often do debilitate people.[13] The second step is to seek to understand why this fact exists. And the third step is practical: truly prudent persons work to preserve the institutions and communities that carry, display, and proclaim the practices which teach wisdom. They also work to change the institutions and communities that undermine the exercises of wisdom and the development of truly wise people. Such a person may not be prudent$_4$; a society may be so shattered that everyone in it may be unable to be fully prudent$_4$. But still this person will seek to change the social structures that block people from making wise choices, taking up good roles, and becoming wise people. Once one is aware that there are social barriers to knowledge and wisdom, like those Code pointed out, one can work to change them where appropriate. The means to be used must be prudent$_3$; Hawkeye Pierce sought to change social conditions and failed miserably because he failed to act prudently.

There is something exceedingly attractive about Swinburne's claim that if "it matters that we have true beliefs, we must seek . . . rational$_5$ beliefs" (1981:73). But if we cannot develop uncontested criteria for discerning rational$_5$ beliefs, how could we develop crieria for recognizing prudent$_5$ agents? Such a goal seems impossible to achieve. Yet that does not imply such goals cannot be *approached* or *desired*. For instance, if one fully warranted a belief, an action, or a practice in an unlimited discourse community, there could be no reason to think that such a belief was not true, the action not moral, or the practice not proper. If one habitually engaged in actions which could be warranted in an unlimited discourse community, they would be indefeasibly warranted. Thus, to the extent that the situation in which one can warrant one's acts approximates what Habermas has called an "ideal speech situation," or to the intense and agonistic discussion Montaigne valorized in "On the art of discussion," to that extent we can begin to understand what a truly and fully wise agent would have to be. To the extent that a tradition, institution, community or practice valorizes the desire to participate in such a seeking for truth in such a situation, to that extent we can recognize a sign that these are wisdom-producing traditions, institutions, communities, or practices. And more important, it may be possible to rule out some candidates for prudence₅ if it can be shown that they could not be warranted in such a situation and it may be possible to show that a prudent₄ person could not participate in some practices because they failed to valorize such seeking for truth.

So what is the practice of wisdom? In short, a truly wise person is one who has learned how to engage wisely in practices that are carried by empowering institutions and learned in enabling communities. One of the constitutive goals of such persons is the creative reproduction of wise practices in all members of the community (and, ideally of all people), and the fostering of institutions and communities that can make that goal a reality. If all that does not obtain, wise people make it their goal. Perhaps we cannot make such a dream real; but it can be a hope that fires our imaginations, lures us to approach it, and draws our commitment.

But if this is the "ideal" of the practice of wisdom, the real world is messier. Conflicts abound, especially religious ones. The questions that we need finally to reach are the ones with which we started: Can a religious commitment be wise? Can a wise person be religious? We are now in position to address these questions.

NOTES TO CHAPTER 4

1. I owe this illustration to Larry Ray Short (1992).

2. In Tilley (1994) I argue that there is good reason to believe that even the "institutional element of religion," often neglected by scholars examining religious practice and belief, is a necessary ingredient even in individuals' religious experience.

3. For critical discussion of these issues, see Tilley 1990, 1992.

4. I appreciate the comments of John McCarthy, Michael Barnes, and Steven Ostovich on an earlier version of this argument. They helped me to see this point more clearly and to revise this argument substantially. Nonetheless, my debt to Swinburne remains intact.

5. Consequentialists could disagree with this. They might say that the consequences of an act, in part, determine the nature of the act, and are thus an essential component of the act. Consequences would thus go far in determining the rightness or wrongness of the act. But this doesn't always apply. Consider a case of a person knowingly having unprotected sex with

an HIV positive partner and not becoming HIV positive therefrom or suffering other significant negative consequences. If that act had no bad consequences, does that mean it likely was wise? Hardly. Consequences are not sufficient to determine the prudence of performing an action. For further discussion of the role of results in determining the nature of an act, specifically of a speech act, see Tilley 1991:20–23, 30–32.

6. Plantinga rejects any deontological "ethic of belief" in part because it is very difficult, and perhaps impossible, for an internalist to specify what one's epistemic duties are in a manner in which people can fulfill them. His argument would not apply to the present "practical" approach because doing what the practice teaches one to do is epistemically external to the individual. If one does what the practice prescribes in developing one's beliefs, one's beliefs are warranted unless some defeating condition obtains—one of which, of course, may be that it is unwise for one to participate in that practice.

Harvey (1979) makes clear that Clifford's epistemic duties do not apply to persons generally, but are duties that apply to persons in specific social roles. Because modern epistemologies, including Plantinga's, are so resolutely general and individualist, they simply cannot account for role-specific practices and duties. Although I cannot argue it here, it seems plausible to say that only when one differentiates practices of knowing can one plausibly introduce acceptable notions of epistemic obligation.

7. I do not use the term "role" lightly. With some exceptions, for example, the role of football fan (as most people take this role), the roles discussed herein are (at least in part) constitutive of the self or the character of the agent (see Tracy 1981: 4 on theologians' roles). Roles and practices are closely related, but not identical. Some roles are institutionally established and required for performing some actions or engaging in some practices. Some acts can be performed or practices undertaken without regard to institutional roles. I develop this point at length with regard to speech acts in my *Evils of Theodicy* (1991:9–81).

8. This discussion has introduced the distinction between "social evils" and an individual's "moral evils," a point that is often obscured by theodicists, not to mention "ordinary" people like Pierce. See Tilley 1991:235–51.

9. Louis Pasteur comes close to being such a revolutionary in medicine by making clear the need for antisepsis. The justices of the American Supreme Court are in a social location where they can change practices substantially, for example, the "Miranda decision," which requires police to inform people they arrest of their rights.

10. This account may seem to involve rejecting an Aristotelian account of prudence, by affirming that prudence is both role specific and person specific. Rather, it gives a different account from Aristotle's of the relationship of prudence to "cunning" or "cleverness." Aristotle's account is based on a hard separation of *deinotes* from *phronesis* (Cf. *Nichomachean Ethics*, 1144b–1145a). This separation seems unwarranted, given his discussion of how virtue is learned (1103a–1105b). How would one learn to be prudent in general except by first learning how to perform particular prudent acts in specific

practices? If these acts are merely clever, how could one learn prudence from performing them or emulating people who habitually perform them?

11. A possible exception may be the arguments among the deaf over whether it would be wise to be able to undergo surgery and therapy that would make hearing possible for a deaf person. Such arguments are extremely interesting, but remain academic in almost all cases, given the state of medical practice. For present purposes, I will ignore them here.

12. In saying this, I am not denying that there are objective moral standards, but claiming that moral claims are warranted not by measuring them against a standard, but by arguing for them in a community of discourse, just as one justifies one's controverted beliefs (if one needs to do so) in a community of discourse while bracketing the controversial question of whether those beliefs are true.

13. This does not imply that social situations and role conflicts are the only cause of people's misery. The incredibility of some Marxists' attempts to warrant such a theory seems to me obvious.

5

The Wisdom of
Religious Commitment

Finally we come to the question of the real focus of this inquiry. How can a wise person make a religious commitment? A wise person is one who has the skill of putting intellect into practice, of making prudent choices about practical matters. To make or to have a religious commitment is to be a person whose character is (at least in part) constituted by participating in the central and distinctive practices (including believing) that constitute a religious tradition. In homelier terms, we can ask how one can wisely "take one's body off to Mass and splash holy water on oneself." How could a Pascal, perhaps, show the interlocutor that such an action was indeed the right, the wise, the prudent, step for her to take? How can we answer, "Should I take up (or keep up) this religious practice, become (or remain) a member of this religious community, take (keep) a place in this institution?"

To answer such questions, a Christian apologist like Pascal would have to show his interlocutor how the undertaking of Christian practices can be wise. But by the definition of religion given in chapter 2, Christianity is not a religion, but a family of religions. Given the argument in chapter 3 detailing the problems of inadequate specificity found in Alston's approach, Christian Mystical Practice is not the issue. We cannot use "Christianity" as our test case, but must turn to a specific form of Christianity, for there are profound practical, communal, and institutional differences between the traditions within Christianity. The "many practices" problem is internal to the family of Christian traditions.

The prudential question is not one for abstract minds, but for embodied persons. It is not about "generic religion" or "classic theism," but about specific practices and the institutional and communal forms of life in which they exist and which are ingredient in them. I have elsewhere argued (Tilley 1994) that the traditional, communal, and institutional elements of a religion are inseparable, even though they are analytically distinguishable (as in chapter 2). Thus, exploring the wisdom of a religious commitment requires attention to all dimensions of a religion.

The question of the wisdom of religious commitment arises concretely only in specific contexts. It is not a question generated by universal skepticism or Cartesian systematic doubt. I take for granted that the approach of "naturalized epistemology," is generally on target. If participants have no reason to doubt the wisdom of their practices, then the question simply does not arise for them. For such thoroughly "once-born" natural believers, religious commitment is an undoubted "given." They are born Buddhists or cradle Catholics. The wisdom of their religious commitment remains transparent for them, unclouded by disconfirming events, testimony, or experiences. There may be absolutely nothing wrong with that epistemically.

"Well, it damned well *should* be clouded!" a cultured despiser of religion or other externalist might reply. But why should it? Because the person has not undertaken to provide foundational warrants for his practice? Why should one do that? Is it because everyone ought not believe any proposition that is not justified or trust any practice that he has not examined and found reliable? That presumes such a high standard of epistemic duty that no one could possibly fulfill it. Such an unreachable universal standard of epistemic duty derailed Clifford's "Ethics of Belief" as indicated in chapter 4. As John Henry Newman put it in that context, "We must take the constitution of the human mind as we find it, and not as we may judge it ought to be" (1870:71).

No one could ever be justified in believing anything (or almost anything) on Clifford's view. However the mind ought to be, it does not work that way in reality. The cultured despiser needs to challenge specific practices and beliefs, specific communities, and specific institutions. In short, if the cultured despiser thinks that a set of religious people or a specific religiously committed person should doubt her religion, the attack will have to be direct and specific: "How can you as a Lutheran believe in an all-powerful, all-good, all-knowing God after Auschwitz?"

Yet insofar as disconfirming evidence or direct attack darkens their commitment, other believers may need to "remake" or confirm it. Still others need to find a new practice. In an era of clashing authorities and rampant cynicism, religious commitment may fade for some and religious practice be abandoned by others. Although I formulate the central question in terms of "making" a commitment, it includes both "remaking" a commitment for those who have come to see other practices and traditions as live options for them and "carrying on" with a commitment one has made.

BASIC WISDOM IN RELIGIOUS COMMITMENT

In line with the discussion of practical wisdom in chapter 4, a person makes a prudent$_1$ act of religious commitment if that act is consistent with her or his beliefs. A religious commitment which is inconsistent with an agent's beliefs is imprudent$_1$.

If you believe that science provides the only ultimate explanation of the way things are in the world, as Antony Flew does, then to participate in any religion that worships, meditates on, or engages in other practices which are in some way involved with responding to a transcendent reality would be imprudent or disingenuous for you. Here the presumptions of a religious commitment would contradict an ultimate belief you held. You cannot sensibly say, "There is no God and I ask Her to bless my venture." The practice of prayer presumes the reality of God; if you have an ultimate belief that there is no God, then you cannot have or make the presumption to engage in the practice.

Of course, you could assume for the sake of argument that God exists and then argue about the propriety of prayer. But then you take for granted the reality of God not to engage in the practice of prayer to God, but to participate in the practice of argument about God. Here your goal is rather different from the practices of prayer or meditation. You might like a good debate or want to explore interesting issues. However, a practical (and at least in some cases, logical) inconsistency emerges if you presume that God does exist when you pray, but you also reject the existence of God. Partaking in a practice is not compatible with rejecting a necessary presumption of the practice.

Yet to commit yourself to a transcendent reality even if the probability of its existence is negligible and even if you think the probability of its existence is negligible, is not necessarily to make an imprudent religious commitment. Chapter 1 showed the significance of Pascal's "wager argument." Its initial step, the calculation of the infinite gain for committed belief, even if it fails to establish the overarching pru-

dence of religious commitment or resolve the problem of "many practices," shows that such a commitment is not imprudent for every
person.

It is possible to pray even if you do not actively believe in God,
but merely hope that God exists (see Tilley 1991:56–63). This attitude
is different from actively disbelieving in God. If you *reject* God, it is
not wise for you to pray to God. If you are agnostic or uncertain about
God, you can pray to God without inconsistency or imprudence—
but if you make a practice of it, perhaps you need to reexamine the
fit between your beliefs and your practices.

Plantinga's argument against metaphysical naturalism, as
sketched in chapter 3, is directly relevant here. First, he claimed that
a naturalized (externalist) epistemology is superior to an internalist
epistemology. Second, as he put it, "naturalistic epistemology flour-
ishes best in the garden of supernaturalistic metaphysics. . . . The
naturalistic epistemologist should therefore prefer theism to metaphysical naturalism" (1993b:237). Thus, the rationally superior position is to be a supernaturalist. I would add that religious commitment
(in general) can be seen as a practical expression of theistic belief.[1] If
it is prudent to make a commitment in line with one's other beliefs,
and if people who accept theism are in a rationally superior position
to those who accept naturalism (like Flew), then a commitment to
theistic practices is prudent$_1$ relative to rationally superior metaphysical beliefs. It may be the case that the question of the wisdom of
religious commitment should come up for any person who wants to
be rational, but arguing that would take us far beyond the issues we
need to examine here.

A prudent$_2$ act of religious commitment is one that follows properly from an agent's assumptions. A religious commitment reached
by using faulty warrants is imprudent$_2$. There may be warrants that
are proper, for example, the voice of authority, or one's religious
experience, given the variety of circumstances in which one engages
in practices and the variety of the practices themselves.[2] One example
would be the story told in chapter 2 of Moshe and the atheist. Moshe
heard the voice of God and responded by acting as God told him to
act. In this case, the experience of the Voice gives warrant to Moshe's
practice and belief. Given the story and given that there are no particular or general defeaters for Moshe's understanding of his experience
(the atheist, you recall, turned up no devices that could have brought
about an illusory experience), then he is prudent to act on his experi-

ence and can even be said to be "called upon" to act on the basis of that experience. Here is a case in which an act of religious commitment follows directly from the person's experience and the beliefs it warrants.[3]

On this account, we can find a place for much contemporary religious epistemology, even if it "plays with" the atheists. It is devoted implicitly to showing that a person's religious commitment is prudent$_1$ or prudent$_2$. These arguments assume that if a belief in God is formed in certain conditions, there is no reasonable criterion that excludes it from being properly basic. Alston argues, as discussed above, that a belief formed in an established doxastic practice is reasonable. These exercises give us good reason to believe that there is no general argument available to show that religious commitment as a type of commitment is imprudent$_2$.

But what of particular religious commitments? The actual issue is not the hypothetical commitments debated by the best minds in academia, but the actual commitments made or avoided by embodied persons in various contexts. That a person has a properly basic religious belief, such as "God speaks to me through this Book," does not itself provide any warrant for taking on the role of a Baptist or a Catholic. Prudence$_1$ and prudence$_2$ in general are so basic, I claimed in chapter 4, that specific practical issues about the wisdom of participating in particular practices don't emerge. The discussion in contemporary religious epistemology also abstracts from the particularity of the agent, her roles, and the institutional, traditional, and communal contexts in which she plays them. In short, their arguments stop at a basic, abstract level which can warrant one's participation in a wide variety of religious traditions as prudent$_2$. Given the Humean shape of the discourse in modern philosophy of religion, religiously committed philosophers have won a substantial battle if they have shown that there is good reason to accept (in general) that (some, but not all) basic religious beliefs are reasonable, and by the "principle of substitutability," that (some, but not all) religious commitments are or at least probably are reasonable and prudent$_{1,2}$.

A person likely believes he is committing himself prudently when his commitment seems prudent$_1$ and prudent$_2$. I am aware of no good argument or examples that show otherwise. One may come to realize that one's act of religious commitment may have been an unhappy one. There may be events or arguments that are potential "defeaters." If they are actual events or sound arguments, they defeat or undermine one's warrant for holding a belief. If I believe a piece of paper is yellow because I look at it and form that belief when I am in a room flooded with yellow light, my warrant for my belief that the paper is yellow is undermined. If someone's argument shows my action in this light, I should recognize that my belief is unwarranted. Presumably, if I am apprised that such a condition did obtain, so that my natural inference from "this looks yellow to me" to "this is yellow" is unwarranted, then I should stop believing the paper is yellow, unless I can check it in white light or undertake other practices to see if my belief can be warranted.

What might undermine or defeat my religious commitment? First, unpleasant accompaniments or unexpected consequences may lead me to reevaluate the prudence of the commitment and lead me to give up my practices. Perhaps religious authorities in whom I believed act heinously and so lose their authoritative position for me (televangelists' financial scandals, divorce among the clergy, or the revelation of a priest's pederasty are examples). Perhaps coming to realize that my religious experience is conditioned by a whole religious culture (tradition, community, institution) will get me to rethink the warrantedness of my beliefs.[4] Perhaps I am overwhelmed by Freud's *Future of an Illusion* assigned as required reading for a university class in religion and come to think that all religious beliefs are illusions. The possibility of reconsidering the practical wisdom of a religious commitment, like the possibility of reconsidering the practical wisdom of a moral choice, is one way that the issues of prudence$_3$ and prudence$_4$ arise.

If it were true that all religious beliefs were Freudian illusions, and I am a religious believer, then my warrant would be defeated (even if I did not realize it). That condition, or others that defeat religious practice and belief, would undermine the reliability of my religious practice and the warrant of the beliefs generated therein. Arguments and evidence might convince me that Freud was right or that other conditions exist that defeat religious practices in general or my practice in particular. It would then be wise to abandon the practice. Just as beliefs can be undermined by "defeaters," so can commitments to practices be undermined.

Epistemologists look for "defeater defeaters," evidence or arguments to show that the defeater does not apply or does not undermine a person's practice and his entitlement to hold a belief. An anti-

Freudian might show that at least some religious practices do not generate irrational illusions to maintain the status quo, but practical convictions that contribute to reforming society. Plantinga's complex argument as sketched in chapter 4 can be seen as a candidate for being a "decisive defeater defeater" as it seeks to show that the skeptics' or Freudians' arguments are not "defeaters" of the practice that generates religious belief or of one's warranted belief in theism.

Yet the present issue is not evidence or arguments that undermine a belief, but those that undermine or threaten to undermine a commitment to a practice. In the arena of pure theory, the fact that arguments can be found to show that an opponent doesn't have a knockdown case against the warrant for your belief may allow you rationally to hold that belief. But in the realm of practical wisdom, the issue is prudential. "Defeaters" may unavoidably raise the question of the prudence of a religious commitment. The problems that arise when the issue is simply one of epistemic entitlement are different from the doubts which arise when the issue is the wisdom of commitment. In the former case, the defensive posture of holding one's position until one is forced to give it up may be appropriate. In the latter case, one may need to search for reasons to keep one's commitments in the face of challenges—which raises issues involved in prudence$_3$.

Here the differences between the academic debate over the reasonableness of religious belief and the actual problems with religious commitment become clear. In the former case, "defeaters" are external challenges to religious belief or to the practices in which they were reliably generated; in the latter, the challenges may be "internal," if not to a specific practice, at least to a person who necessarily engages in many practices in different social locations. Perhaps one might think of such states of affairs or circumstances as spiritual deserts, as dark nights, or as tests of faith. But why should one think that such challenges are simply *tests* of commitment?

Second, overwhelming disconfirming evidence might undermine one's commitment. If you were a Jew interned in a Nazi concentration camp, the academics' assurances that you were epistemically entitled to hold fast to your belief in God would be small comfort. Your guards might literally beat that belief out of you. Elie Wiesel (1960) once portrayed the destruction of his religious practice when he was a young man in the death camps:

Some talked of God, of his mysterious ways, of the sins of the Jewish people and of their future deliverance. But I had ceased to pray. How I sympathized with Job! I did not deny God's existence, but I doubted His absolute justice. . . . (42)

Thousands of voices repeated the benediction; thousands of men prostrated themselves like trees before a tempest.

"Blessed be the Name of the Eternal!"

Why, but why should I bless Him? In every fiber I rebelled. Because He had had thousands of children burned in His pits. Because He kept six crematories working night and day, on Sundays and feast days? Because in His great might He had created Auschwitz, Birkenau, Buna, and so many factories of death? How could I say to Him: "Blessed art Thou, Eternal, Master of the Universe, Who chose us from among the races to be tortured day and night, to see our fathers, our mothers, our brothers, end in the crematory? Praised be Thy Holy Name, Thou Who hast chosen us to be butchered on Thine altar?" . . . (64)

My neighbor, the faceless one, said:

"Don't let yourself be fooled with illusions. Hitler has made it very clear that he will annihilate all the Jews before the clock strikes twelve, before they can hear the last stroke."

I burst out:

"What does it matter to you? Do we have to regard Hitler as a prophet?"

His glazed, faded eyes looked at me. At last he said in a weary voice:

"I've got more faith in Hitler than in anyone else. He's the only one who's kept his promises, all his promises, to the Jewish people"(76–77).

Wiesel's extreme case helps us see that the real issue is not defending entitlement to believe, or questions about the proper environment for our properly functioning cognitive faculties, but the possibility and the prudence of maintaining a religious commitment in the face of massive disconfirmation.

Although reformed epistemologists have shown that people believing religiously are not irrational, and I have claimed above that their arguments can at least show that certain religious commitments are not unwise at a basic level, more is required. Doubts, whether well- or ill-founded, do arise for religious believers. These doubts are not epistemological "defeaters," but questions and problems that are generated by a person's participating in the practices that constitute one's life—especially if that life is lived in desperation and degradation.

Third, "interpractice" conflicts may arise. Save for those rare people who are isolated from the nonreligious communities of the world in cloistered convents, people in a pluralistic society play many roles and participate in many practices. Consider George Bernard Shaw's witticism, "A catholic university is a contradiction in terms." Whatever verisimilitude it has is due to the fact that the practices that constitute being a good Catholic and those that constitute being a good scholar have rather different "moralities of knowledge" (Harvey 1966:102) or "divergent plausibility structures" (Tracy 1981:26). The basic standard practice for Catholics is to presume faith and seek understanding; the basic standard practice for the university scholar is to question all presumptions and accept only those that can be rationally validated. Thus, the conflict.

But consider those who are practicing Catholics, and practicing scholars, in a secular university. They participate in two profoundly different practices, sustained in rather different communities, and carried in different institutions. Both roles are constitutive, in part, of their characters (see chapter 2). Like most people in this society, they internalize practical conflicts whether they like it or not. The ruthless lawyer is also a caring mother. The scheming politician is also a practicing Quaker. The Disciple of Christ is an air force colonel. We live in a culture in which we give our embodied selves to many contrasting and sometimes conflicting practices. We may be able to seal our beliefs into watertight compartments in our minds, but we cannot seal our practices into watertight compartments in our lives. We may try to keep our religious practices confined to that fraction of the week that is a Sunday worship hour and our other practices out of it, but that is religious hypocrisy. We are people who are open to interpractice overlaps. We are open to the possibility—and for many of us the actuality—that what we warrantedly believe through participating in one practice conflicts or contrasts with what we warrantedly believe through participating in other practices. We can call this the "problem of interpracticality." It is not merely an external problem of circumstances which defeat our practice. It is a problem internal to our lives and potentially explosive.

Of course, for some this seems not to be a problem. The solution is simply to order one's practices. Perhaps one practice has an overriding rule, "if there is an insoluble conflict in practices, give up the others." But this solution simply won't do. First, more than one practice could easily have such rules. Second, no algorithm or rule can tell us how to apply the rule. The prudent move in such a conflict might be to give up the practice with the overriding rule, rather than the practice that conflicts with it. It is a problem for practical judgment, not for rule-following behavior.

One possible solution to the problem of ordering might be "intratextualist" (see Lindbeck 1984). Christians may conform all their beliefs to the rules the Christian tradition has generated from one "narrative," for example, the scriptural story from genesis to apocalypse with the story of Jesus as its determining center. One does not engage in the practice of interpreting that narrative to those who "live outside it." In a culture that celebrates the death of God, what good would such interpretation do? Rather, one makes one's home within a community that dwells within the text; the text is one's overarching myth (see chapter 2); it shapes one's understanding of whatever there is. Beyond the obvious question of "why this narrative?" an intratextualist solution founders when confronted with our actual practices, the differing social and historical locations Christians have had, and the beliefs they particularly generate (see Tilley 1989). Like it or not, the pure intratextualist fails to note that "the line between the church and the world passes right through each Christian heart" (McClendon 1986:17). Pure intratextualism founders on the fact that there is no one overarching story for Christians to dwell in, no single set of practices that determine Christianity, no sacred canopy in which to dwell. Even if a framework of rules can be drawn from most of them, it cannot tell us how to apply these rules in novel circumstances— that is a problem of practical wisdom.[5] Because "intratextualist" approaches founder, there is no model for a solution to the problem of interpracticality to be found in a pure intratextualist approach.

Further, the intratextualist typically attends to the community and to the tradition, but neglects the institutional element of religion (see Thiel 1991), though some of the conflicting practices derive from a person's institutional role, status, or office. Suppose for example, that a biblical scholar teaching in a seminary of a denomination that teaches the literal inerrancy of the Bible comes to realize that such a position is untenable. What is such a scholar to do in the classroom: teach the doctrine of inerrancy? Teach the doctrine and simultaneously undermine it? Present the doctrine and the reasons for disagreeing with it? The problem is generated by the insoluble tension between the scholar's new convictions and the specific institutional role the scholar plays. Intratextual approaches have nothing to say about such conflicts because the text provides no way to resolve role-specific conflicts between practices within a religion.[6]

Moreover, when one considers not merely texts to be "dwelt in," but the conflicts generated because no one practice is sufficient to sustain human life in modern and contemporary culture, even the attempt to "order" practices in conflict becomes exceedingly difficult. If I cannot give up my work as a butcher, must I abandon Buddhism? If I know no marketable skill other than bootlegging to support my family, must I abandon the Southern Baptist tradition? If I am a colonel in charge of a combat division, must I give up a church that preaches the Sermon on the Mount? Even if in some way a text determines the meaning-world of one's life, one cannot live within one practice, that is, "intrapractically."

In summary, the unpleasant concomitants or consequences of some commitments, the problem of massively disconfirming evidence, and the actual problems of interpracticality generate questions pointing to our need for understanding whether our commitments to the practices that shape and form us even as we practice them are prudent$_3$.

THE PRACTICAL PURSUIT OF RELIGIOUS WISDOM

As with the display of practical wisdom in the last chapter, so the problems now become more complex and more particular in this chapter. We need to examine a specific tradition, a specific test case. Although any tradition could be used, I will turn to Roman Catholicism and to the wisdom of being a theologian in that religious context (not surprising, given my social location). The theologian is a person who almost inevitably faces the problem of interpracticality, and thus makes a good exemplar for understanding the wisdom of religious commitment as we enter the complex area of "role-specific" prudence. Three assumptions lie behind the analysis of this section, which would also apply analogously to traditions other than Roman Catholicism.

First, I assume that insofar as the practice of theology has an inclusive goal, the inclusive duty of the Catholic theologian is to show the wisdom of commitment to Catholicism.[7] The question Pascal's interlocutor asks is, finally, a theological as well as a practical one. The person whose practice is devoted to answering it is the theologian. It is the overarching "role-specific responsibility" for theologians given their social locations. Obviously, theologians have responsibilities other than showing that commitment in and to their traditions is wise, duties dependent on the demands of the specific disciplines in which they have practical competence. Especially when undertaking exegetical, historical, or cross-cultural investigations, or when working with scholars from other traditions, theologians probably have no specific duty to show the wisdom of participating in their tradition. After all, a person cannot do everything at once and in some academic roles, one's own theological and religious commitments may become practically irrelevant.[8]

However, these practices tie individual theologians to the wider responsibilities borne by other theologians from their own community, theorists from other traditions, and scholars of religion generally. Thus, theologians may contribute to the inclusive duty of the theologian indirectly, rather than directly, by their research and teaching practices. In pursuing responsibilities in specific areas, theologians have direct role-specific duties that do not require explicit attention to the inclusive responsibility of theologians. These practices make rather different demands on the theologians.

In some sense, every participant has the "duty" to show the wisdom of one's commitment to a tradition. Believers may not be able to give an account of the wisdom of their practices. However, as believers, they show their wisdom, whether or not they have "role-specific responsibilities" to defend the faith by argument. It falls on the shoulders of theologians to give such an account—or to make one available to them.

Second, I assume that each theologian fulfills this duty by engaging in various practices, relative to the people with whom, and the places in which, each works. Theologians do research alone and in collaboration with other theologians and scholars from other disciplines. They inform and engage in dialogue with church officials and non-Catholic scholars. They educate undergraduates in colleges and universities. They instruct seminarians. They direct graduate students. They worship (and may preach) in chapel or church or base community. The ways in which they present or exemplify the wisdom of commitment to Christianity will vary with their relationships with others. For instance, preparing and instructing seminarians to become leaders of local ecclesial communities and officials in an enduring institution is different from liberally educating undergraduates, who may or may not be Christians. Both of these differ from responsibility for enabling students to become colleagues, which is the purpose of graduate education. Theologians, like other academics, have different responsibilities to different people depending on their relationships. But unlike some academics, theologians (at least in the North American context) have more than one type of professional "social location," more than one primary professional reference group, and a wider variety of practices to engage in because in the North American context the explanatory, hermeneutical, and theological approaches to studying religion and religiosity are intertwined.

Third, I assume, following David Tracy (1981), that theologians properly work in a number of social locations. Tracy finds three types of "social location" or discourse communities, the church, the academy, and the wider society (including technical, cultural and political components). This variety can create problems for theologians. As Tracy put it, "Each of us seems to become not a single self but several selves at once. Each speaks not merely to several publics external to the self but to several internalized publics in one's own reflections on authentic existence" (1981:4). Tracy's noting that the theologian is "several selves at once" seems absolutely right. However, Tracy tends to identify the social location of the "church" with the institutional church. But the church is not only institution, but also community, as noted in chapter 2. We need also to attend to the local communities in which traditions are transmitted, including, for example, parishes, base communities, and devotional societies. Thus, I would add a fourth general sort of "public," and yet another "role-informed self," for the theologian: the theologian belongs to local communities as well as an enduring institution.[9]

The varying demands of these roles for and on theologians may create serious tensions for them. They may realize the distinctions between the social spaces in which they work, but well be unable to separate the habits they learn in each. Theologians are embodied persons, engaging in actual practices, not disembodied minds who can build watertight compartments for isolating beliefs. The social reality of the theologian is that of "an intellectual related to three publics, socialized in each, internalizing their sometimes divergent plausibility structures, in a symbiosis [exceedingly] personal, complex and sometimes unconscious" (Tracy 1981:26). In sum, I assume (1) that theologians generally carry out their inclusive duty of showing the wisdom of commitment to a specific tradition and their role-specific duties to the other members of their community, (2) that these role-specific duties vary (and may conflict with each other) according to the personal and professional practices theologians engage in, and (3) that these role-specific duties vary (and may conflict with each other) according to the social locations of these relationships. Indeed if Tracy is correct, the nature of the "symbiosis" may show whether a theologian can be a prudent person, a crucial issue in constructing a practical philosophy of religion.

In line with the argument in chapter 4, a prudent$_3$ commitment is one that is prudent$_2$ and whose assumptions and warrants of inference have been checked to an adequate degree, given the person's role-specific obligations and circumstances. Relevant considerations are (a) the probability or propriety of the person's assumptions and warrants, and (b) a proper delineation of the significance of the commitment. An imprudent$_3$ religious commitment is one for which a person has not properly checked her or his assumptions, inferential warrants, or the significance of the commitment.

(a) A prudent$_3$ religious commitment requires appropriate checking of the person's factual assumptions and/or probability beliefs. A religious commitment is imprudent$_3$ if it is based on demonstrably erroneous assumptions (e.g., a person who came to believe in the reality of the Great Pumpkin as a result of reading "Peanuts" cartoons by Charles Schulz). However, the mode and extent of appropriate investigation is situation and role specific. As noted above in discussing prudent$_3$ acts in general, this level brings in traditional, institutional, and communal components.

The question of the wisdom of one's religious commitments may seldom arise, and the three problems noted above may never occur. Norman Malcolm (1977) has even argued that religious believing is a practice as justifiably groundless as a person's believing that her or his name is "N. N." He claims, in effect, that our practices bring about such beliefs. My belief about my name is contingently true, but, unlike other contingent beliefs, is not falsifiable for me. It is contingently true—I might have had another name. But unlike common sense and scientific beliefs (which I can falsify by engaging in the practices of common sense or scientific investigation), that belief is not falsifiable for me. It would make no difference to say whether I cannot or do not check my belief.

Malcolm takes this sort of belief as parallel to religious belief (186–90).[10] Just as religious beliefs arise in and from religious practices, so one's belief that her name is N. N. arises from the practice of being named and called N. N. However, one can imagine rare situations in which one might investigate one's name and allow the results of investigation to change one's belief about one's name (e.g., a person discovering he was adopted might find a new name, or one recovering from amnesia might have to try to find out what her name is). Similarly, one might be unable to pray to God and come to discover it is Hitler rather than God who truly kept his promises to one, if one were an interned Jew.

Malcolm makes the seemingly odd claim that it makes no difference whether we say we cannot or simply do not check our religious beliefs. The point he makes clear is that the question of "checking" is not ordinarily part of the practice of believing religiously. However, when we are in circumstances in which there is cause to question our commitments, such as circumstances in which our practice is challenged or upset, we can and do engage in the practice of checking because we must. If we must do so, then it must be possible to do so without violating the full commitment that seems to be a component of specifically religious commitment. Carrying out a religious commitment or holding a belief are different practices from checking them, but these cannot be incompatible.

Individuals may have as little control over whether they question their religious practices and beliefs as over whether they forget their names. Wiesel certainly did not seek the circumstances that gave rise to his inability to pray and his doubts about God's justice. Believers do not seek to live in a culture that undermines religious commitment. Just as beliefs are not ordinarily directly within our voluntary control, so doubts may arise without our desiring or willing them.

The possibility and the obligation for a wise religious person to check a religious commitment or belief thus arises only in certain situations. Prudent people normally do not go around looking for occasions to investigate their practices. "Why look for trouble?" Nor should they, unless they have a role-specific duty to do so. They properly should presume their beliefs warranted, their practices reliable, their cognitive equipment functioning properly unless they have reason to doubt their presumptions. Thus, for most religious participants, thoughtfully accepting the traditions of the religious community in which they were socialized, acknowledging the authority of an institutional leader, accepting the grace of a conversion, following an intuition, developing insights through meditation, finding a sense of ultimate at-homeness, etc., are practices that provide good warrants for continuing a religious commitment or making one, assuming these commitments were and remain prudent$_1$ and prudent$_2$. Most religious believers properly assume that the beliefs which they developed through engaging in the practices of their tradition are correct, although they may not be able to defend their practices or beliefs fully against skeptical attack. Commitment in such a context is normally not imprudent.

Religious commitment is often attacked as imprudent because, upon academic reflection, it is alleged to be irrational. This attack is a special circumstance that has become academically generalized. Defending religious belief in this context is a role-specific responsibility of the theologian, which can be carried out by constructing philosophical and theological arguments. It may best be understood as a necessary part of a theologian's inclusive duties in a society in which cultured despisers attack religious belief in general or seek to undermine belief in God. The theological and philosophical arguments thus constructed may be sufficient to show that a prudent$_3$ person can make a theistic religious commitment. And in this context the generic defenses or apologetics typical of the academic philosophy of religion, such as those discussed in chapter 3, may be the best strategy a philosophical theologian can follow.

Religious beliefs can also be undermined when a religious believer comes to a crisis of faith. The commitment one had made comes to be questioned. In so doing, the believer is raising the question of the prudence$_3$ of making a religious commitment and may turn to the theologian as a guide. A teacher in an ecclesial community is obliged to investigate the assumptions of that community and the warrants a person can use in making a religious commitment. The theologian must provide help in understanding the religious community, distinguishing religious conversions from brainwashing, differentiating misleading from illuminating intuitions, recognizing beliefs warranted only by wishing they were true, and sharing the results of such investigations with others, etc.

Theologians do not respond solely to "external" or contextual challenges. As a religious tradition incarnates itself in novel times and places, internal difficulties often arise for people who live in the communities dedicated to the tradition. When these difficulties become acute and affect a people, theologians may propose resolutions to the problems. Indeed, much theological debate can be seen as exploring (and sometimes advocating) a specific way out of unavoidable difficulties or conflicts which appeals to the "text" or the tradition finally cannot resolve. Theologians must investigate, not assume, the assumptions and warrants ingredient in ordinary religious commitments. Ordinary believers are "ordinary" not because they are mediocre or haphazard in practice or belief, but because they do not have a role specific duty to check the cogency of the tradition. They appropriately rely on theologians and other religious authorities who have such a role to perform this check. Ordinary believers can thus assume that the committed scholars who participate in the ongoing tradition can defend and explicate the tradition and thus show that they are not imprudent$_3$ to be committed to the tradition. Thus theologians carry out their role-specific duties for other members of a religious community.[11]

(b) Religious commitments are imprudent$_3$ if the significance of the commitment for the life of the believer is not clearly delineated. For example, a vow made in the absence of an understanding of how making the vow will affect one's life is imprudent. People may make sacramental marriage vows of life-long care and fidelity without sufficiently realizing the extent of the obligations they undertake. Candidates for a Roman Catholic religious order may take vows of poverty, chastity, and obedience without any inkling of the extent to which their own inclinations may have to be thwarted in the future. Such vows may not only be imprudent, but also invalid. Seekers may join a cult and receive intense satisfaction and acceptance without realizing that they have turned control of their lives over to a religious leader. In each of these cases, the sort of commitment made is imprudent$_3$; in some cases, the lack of understanding may be profound enough so that it may later be said that one had made no vow at all or that the cultist had been brainwashed. The conditions for justifying such claims is not our concern here, but recognition that vows can sometimes be annulled in the Roman Catholic Church and cultists can sometimes be deprogrammed suggest that the imprudence$_3$ of some religious commitments is recognized.

The responsibility for a person's not realizing the significance of a religious belief and thus making an imprudent$_3$ religious commitment may vary. A trusted teacher or religious leader may have failed to make clear the significance of the commitment. A person may not have been able to see the scope or the significance of the commitment. But whatever the cause and the assignment of responsibility, a religious commitment made without a clear delineation of its significance for the life of the believer is imprudent$_3$.

The theologian bears a specific responsibility for determining what the consequences of a commitment are. However, it may well be the duty of the person's teachers (whether theologian, religious educator, pastor, spouse, parent, friend) to communicate the implications of commitment to the ordinary believer. In this sense, theologians have the role of "resource persons" for the institution and the community.

The theologian bears a specific responsibility for accounting for overwhelming disconfirming evidence. Catholic political theologian Johann Baptist Metz (1981) made the sort of task the theologian must accomplish as clear as anyone:

> At the end of 1967 there was a round-table discussion in Münster between Czech philosopher Machovec, Karl Rahner, and myself. Toward the end of the discussion, Machovec recalled Adorno's saying: "After Auschwitz, there are no more poems." . . . Machovec cited Adorno's saying and asked me if there could be for us Christians, after Auschwitz, any more prayers. I finally gave the answer which I would still give today: We can pray *after* Auschwitz, because people prayed *in* Auschwitz (18–19).

That religious practice can be a response to horrible suffering is clear. Whether some practice is a wise one or one that is "opiating" in the Marxist sense needs to be examined in concrete circumstances. But the real religious responses are ones in which members of a tradition form a community of solidarity and resistance to engage in practices which counteract and interrupt evils and help heal and console victims, not one in which a theodicy whitewashes God and the evils in God's world (see Tilley 1991; Welch 1985, 1990). The theologian bears the responsibility of showing such practices possible; the community bears the burden of making them actual.

The theologian must also deal with the problems of interpracticality. However, as suggested above in the example of the biblical scholar in a denomination that avows inerrancy, it is at this point that the theologians' problems become acute. Unpleasant concomitants or consequences can afflict anyone. Overwhelming disconfirming evidence may undermine anyone's commitments. But the problem of interpractical conflicts is especially acute for theologians because showing how interpractice conflicts can be overcome is a role-specific duty of the theologian. If the theologian cannot show how this conflict can be resolved in practice, then the problem of interpracticality is one that can undermine the wisdom of commitment to the tradition. If the theologian is not or cannot be a truly prudential agent, then the ordinary believer who relies on the theologian partakes in a practice that the theologian (who has the role-specific responsibility to do so) cannot show to be one to which a truly prudent agent can be committed.

Adapting the work of chapter 4, a prudent$_4$ religious commitment can be seen as one made by a prudent$_4$ agent, a person who acts in conformity with the standards appropriate to the agent's stations, positions, or roles. An imprudent$_4$ religious commitment is one made by an agent who fails, consciously or not, to act in conformity with the agent's roles. Can a prudent person make a religious commitment?

In the abstract the obvious answer seems to be "yes." A person may engage in various practices. If each of these have different internal standards and different goals, then the answer is an almost unquestionable "yes." There seems no reason to think, for example, that a good nurse or bricklayer, a good parent or child, a good republican or revolutionary, could not also be a good Baptist or Buddhist. Of course, specific role inconsistencies or interpractical problems can arise. A prudent Southern Baptist in a teetotal strand of that tradition would not be wise to be a bootlegger; a bootlegger who was a member of a teetotal Baptist assembly would be either disingenuous or unwise. And it might seem imprudent for someone to abandon all his or her other roles to follow a charismatic leader. But in actual life it is specific roles and their potential conflicts with which we have to deal.

Theologians should show or display a religious commitment to be prudent$_4$. In effect, for them to show that a prudent$_4$ person can make a religious commitment requires showing that a specific commitment can be made consistently by persons who habitually check their assumptions and warrants for their beliefs and choices, given their role-specific responsibilities. To show a religious commitment imprudent$_4$ is to show that it cannot be made by persons who habitually and properly check their assumptions and warrants for their beliefs and choices, given their role-specific responsibilities. These arguments and the claims they seek to warrant are not properly ingredient in holding a religious belief or making a religious commitment, but they are properly theological. Only those with the role-specific duties of theologians need to make them.

Here the different roles of ordinary religious believers and theologians become explicit. Ordinary believers do not have role-specific duties to check on the warrants for their beliefs. They should be prudent$_1$ and prudent$_2$ in their religious commitments. However, except to the extent that circumstances raise questions for them, they do not have the obligation of defending their religious commitments as prudent$_3$. They can rely on those members of their community who do theology to enable them to *have* prudent$_3$ assumptions and warrants for their religious commitments and to provide them assistance, directly or indirectly, when they need to defend the wisdom of their commitment. Their roles as members of the community require that they engage in the practices that make community—"communitas"—actual. If those problems are resolved, and if the ordinary believer is wise in her various roles, then she can be a prudent$_4$ person when she makes a religious commitment.

If a religious tradition generates a common pattern of inconsistent role-specific responsibilities in making a religious commitment, then a prudent$_4$ person should (at least *prima facie*) avoid making a religious commitment. It would be unwise to commit oneself to a tradition that generates deep-seated internal conflicts. If the theologian's roles generate such a pattern, then a theologian cannot be a prudent$_4$ person. If theologians cannot be prudent$_4$ persons, then they are in no position to show how a prudent$_4$ person can make a commitment to the practices that constitute the tradition. They cannot properly engage in the religious practices that constitute their roles as ordinary believers and do their duty toward the other members of the community.

As noted above, theologians' roles—and selves—are constituted by varied relationships in multiple social locations. As members of the academy, theologians have different responsibilities. These may seem to place them in tension with their responsibilities as religious believers or teachers, as Tracy notes. While an ordinary believer may justly assume the prudence$_3$ of religious commitment unless there is reason to doubt it, the theologian has a role-specific duty to investigate the assumptions and warrants ingredient in those commitments. If the assumptions appear to be inappropriate, the theologian has a duty to question them. Theologians may not be able to establish the cogency of assumptions and inferences, but must be able to defend them, as part of their duty to the community. Those assumptions that are indefensible must be relinquished as supporting imprudent$_3$ religious commitments. Those that are held despite their conflict with the standards for assumptions in other areas may be prudent$_3$, but not prudent$_4$.

Investigating religious claims may place the theologian qua theologian in tension with others in the religious institution or community and in tension with oneself qua one's role as a member of the community and an officer of the institution. Theologians have role-specific responsibilities to those with whom they work in their multiple social locations (and, in a sense, to the selves they have become through their multiformed socialization). But if theologians are to be prudent$_4$, these tensions must not be insuperable. If the theologian's role-specific responsibilities are insolubly or essentially conflicted, then a prudent$_4$ person cannot be a theologian. To put it briefly and bluntly, "academic theologian" cannot be an oxymoron as "Buddhist butcher" is.

In defining religion in chapter 2, I paid special attention to distinguishing the institutional, communal, and traditional elements in a religion. In the Roman Catholic Church, recent public struggles between the Congregation for the Doctrine of the Faith (CDF) and Hans Küng, Leonardo Boff, Charles Curran, and others illustrate the tensions between the varied roles that theologians play. Each of these theologians has carried out the role-specific duties of researchers, working in the college, university, or seminary. Each investigated assumptions and warrants for aspects of contemporary Catholic teaching. Each investigated and responded to external challenges to or internal difficulties in the lived tradition of Roman Catholicism. In doing so, they have sometimes been perceived by institutional authorities as challenging orthodoxy while also being seen by members of the academy as responsible and effective scholars.

The results they achieve in their practice as scholars have, in effect, led officials of the CDF to render an institutionally authoritative judgment that their research has brought them to conclusions in conflict with contemporary orthodoxy. As a result, these theologians have been removed, directly or indirectly, from their roles as institutionally designated teachers in and for the Roman Catholic community.[12] Their specific investigations have been declared in conflict with the overarching goal of the theologian: to show the wisdom of commitment to Catholicism. The CDF officials have the institutional authority to determine whether the Catholic community's theologians are in conformity with the Catholic tradition. They also have the authority to impose some sanctions within the community. In short, given the pattern of this specific religious tradition, significant conflicts between role-specific responsibilities can be and have been generated.

The upshot of this is that the CDF has acted institutionally in a way that undercuts the possibility that critical theologians can be prudent$_4$. That is, it is the considered judgment of the institutional authorities in the CDF that these theologians cannot be prudent$_3$ in all the roles they play. There seems, then, to be an inherent contradiction, not only a tension, between being a prudent$_3$ theologian in the Catholic Church and a prudent$_3$ theologian in the academy. Harvey has argued that the "moralities of knowledge" (1966) or "role-specific obligations" (1979) are rather different; in present terms, these would be contrasting or conflicting practices ensconced in differing social locations. The CDF actions seem to be institutional validation of the incompatibility of being members of both religious and academic communities with their contrasting practices.

These actions suggest that it might not be possible for a prudent$_4$ theologian to make a commitment to Roman Catholicism. That is, the theologian would not be able to show that ordinary believers could be wise in their own commitments. Hans Küng has retained his role as a professor in the University of Tübingen by being dissociated from the Catholic theological faculty and ensconced in an ecumenical research institute. Charles Curran has been deprived of his *jus mandatum*, fired from his position at Catholic University, and now holds a chair at Southern Methodist University. Leonardo Boff has resigned from the priesthood and the Franciscan order. Other theologians, recognized by fellow theologians as leading scholars, including Bernard Häring and Edward Schillebeeckx, have testified to the untoward stress under which the CDF investigations and actions have placed them. All of these examples indicate that the conflict between their roles as officers in the institution (priest-theologians) and as serious academics who work to explicate the tradition were insurmountable without significant changes in the roles they played and the locations in which they constituted themselves as theologians. They have not abandoned their religious heritage, as did Ernst Renan, Alfred Loisy, William Sullivan, and others when Roman Catholic "modernism" was crushed early in this century. However, role specific conflicts have caused many of them to abandon (sometimes unwillingly) their roles in and for their Catholic community and institution.

These facts suggest that it is possible, that a prudent$_4$ person could not make a religious commitment within the Catholic tradition, for, as we saw in chapter 4, a prudent$_4$ agent does not seek to undertake roles whose duties conflict. That would leave ordinary Catholics in a devastating position. They might be able to see or show that their religious commitments were not imprudent acts, but could not show how they could be prudent agents, for the members of their community who have the role-specific responsibility to do so have had the results of their work undermined. The result would be equivalent to fideism, at best, a "credo quia absurdum" at worst. The latter are intolerable (Penelhum 1983:40–61; 117). It would be absurd for theologians or other authorities to delight in an inability to show that a prudent$_4$ person can make a religious commitment. The former would seem inconsistent with the traditional refusal of Catholic theologians (not to mention the decrees of Vatican I) to separate faith from reason. Such a fideist strategy might be sufficient to defend a believer's rationality or to show her commitment prudent$_2$. But, if generalized, fideism would encourage radical relativism, theological reductionism, and religious indifferentism.

Theologians who accepted this view would be in an intolerable situation. They would have no way to show the prudence of any religious commitment since the causes for accepting any would not be a matter of rationality or prudence, but merely a matter of taste or training. The radical relativist could show no one to be mistaken, no view implausible, no commitment imprudent. Such a tactic should be avoided. A theologian shows a religious commitment prudent$_4$ to the extent that it can be made by a person who acts in conformity with the standards appropriate to all one's roles. A theologian shows a religious commitment imprudent$_4$ if the warrants and inferences needed to support it fail to meet role-appropriate standards. But it may be the case that the institutional authorities in Roman Catholicism may show that it is imprudent$_4$ to be both a Catholic theologian and an academic.

Practices are role-specific. If there are irreconcilable conflicts between practices in which we *choose* to engage, then the wise thing to do may be to abandon one of the practices. One cannot abandon a universal or practically universal practice. If, for example, there were an irreconcilable conflict between a specific practice and perceptual practice, one might be prudent to abandon the specific practice. If one is a theologian, and the conflict between religious commitment and commitment to the standards of argument and investigation in academia seemed irreconcilable, one wise path to take (although not the only one) would be to abandon one or the other. But if one had to do so, it would indicate that one could not see a way to be both a Catholic theologian and an academic. Thus, it would seem that such a combination could not be prudent$_4$.

The fact that some faithful theologians are not prudent$_4$ religious believers and are forced to give up a significant role that constitutes their agency indicates that these conflicts can be debilitating. The roles theologians take and the practices they engage in create conflicting demands on them. But this situation is not hopeless. In chapter 4, I claimed that recognizing such social facts was the first step to take to get around the wall blocking access to "universal wisdom" while avoiding the swamp of relativism. We have done that: the social facts are sometimes painful. The second step is to find out why these facts exist.

The all too typical answers to this question focus, alas, on abuses. Conservatives see progressive theologians as undermining the faith. Liberals see the hand of authority as fearful and excessive. Whether the theologians named above or the official authorities abused their roles or positions is not directly to the point. We need to avoid beginning with abuses—they may be the symptoms, not the disease.

Philosopher of religion Friedrich von Hügel (1904) identified a necessary connection and tension between official authority and living religion. Writing at the heart of the modernist crisis in Roman Catholicism, where the tension between progressive theologians and integralist authorities would eventually reach the breaking point, he found that the tension between the conservative official authority and the progressive explorer in religion was necessary for a tradition to live. He wrote of the theologians (among others) and their relationship to authority:

> The lonely, new and daring (if but faithful, reverent and loving) outgoing of the discoverer and investigator are as truly acts of, are as necessary parts of, the Church and her life as his coming back to the Christian hive and community, which latter will then gradually test his contribution by tentative applications to its own life, and will in part assimilate, in part simply tolerate, in part finally reject it. And such a lonely, venturesome outgoing appears, in all kinds of degree and form, in every sort of life. The inventive, often most daring, ever at first opposed, philanthropy of the Saints belongs entirely to this exploratory, pioneer class of action in the rhythmic "inspiration-expiration" life, in

the breathing of the living Church. The Church is thus, ever and everywhere, both progressive and conservative; both reverently free-lance and official; both . . . creative and reproductive; both daring to the verge of presumption and prudent to the verge of despair. And Church officials are no more the whole Church or a complete specimen of the average of the Church than Scotland Yard or the War Office or the House of Lords, though admittedly necessary parts of national life, are the whole, or average samples, of the life and fruitfulness of the English nation. The true cure here would then be for the officials to cultivate in themselves also the non-official, the out-going, lonely and daring, the "expiration" movement of the complete soul and community; and for the pioneers and investigators to keep alive in themselves the recognition and practice of the homing, the "inspiration" movement, the patient referring back and living with the slow-moving, mentally ruminating, socially regulative multitude, and its and their official heads (16–17).

Von Hügel's insight is that the different moralities of knowledge, varied role-specific obligations, or divergent plausibility structures are necessary constituents for a living, not fossilized, religious tradition. Not only is an institution necessary for a community to pass on a tradition, but members of that community must also find ways to reshape the community, reform the institution, and extend that tradition. Religious communities can relax into complacency, institutional authorities can construct their authority so that they gain tremendous power or prestige (which an ideology critique pursued by others can reveal), and religious practices can become rote and meaningless. A religion is neither a text nor set of doctrines nor a set of rituals, but a living, breathing body that must change if it is to live. Each of its constituents must change—Newman's motto, "Growth the evidence of life," is obviously relevant to religion. The tensions are necessary ones if a religion is to live and not be a fossilized tradition, an empty community, and a hollow institution. The tensions exist because they are necessarily parts of every enduring religion. We err badly if we think that either the brave religious explorers or the stodgy official authorities represent "real Catholicism." Catholicism, like any religion, is not reducible to either.

What this means is that the third step, the practical step, is not to abolish tensions, for instance, by getting rid of institutional authorities. That is not possible. Not only could a religion not exist without them, but a *healthy* religion needs the tensions authorities and explorers create. Rather, if these tensions become debilitating, prudent theologians take practical steps with more nuanced goals. They work to preserve the empowering and root out the debilitating tensions. Such a theologian may not be able to be prudent$_4$. A religion may be torn apart by hidden tensions in its members so that no official authority or exploring theologian could be prudent$_4$. But the prudent theologian works to reform the institution, to reunderstand the tradition, and to succor the community. The only wise alternative is to give up the whole project and admit that one can no longer find hope within the religion. At least on the face of things, both sorts of options, becoming an agent for reform within the tradition or abandoning the tradition, seem acts a prudent$_4$ theologian might perform.

How could one approach the goal of discerning what the more prudent path to walk is? Given the problems with level five of Swinburne's rationality calculus and of the portryal of prudential complexity developed in chapter 4, the only possibility for such discernment seems to be for theologians to engage in a conversation in an unlimited community of discourse such as sketched by Habermas. The discourse community would have to be able to engage in the sort of agonistic conversation sketched brilliantly by Montaigne as cited in chapter 1, especially to avoid the "lazy tolerance" typical of modernity. If one engaged in the practice of fully warranting one's claim to be prudent$_4$ in an unlimited discourse community, there could be no reason to think that one wouldn't be a prudent person. Thus, to the extent that the situation in which a theologian can show a religious commitment prudent$_4$ in a situation that approximates an ideal speech situation, to that extent the theologian's religious commitments can be justifiably presumed to be prudent. To the extent that a theologian cannot show a religious commitment prudent$_4$ in a situation approximating an ideal speech situation, to that extent the theologian's religious commitments cannot be presumed to be prudent.

How could theologians do that? First, they would have to show that the tradition, community, and institution that constituted their religion was open to validation in an unlimited discourse situation, and they would have to be committed to forming such a discourse. For example, the Catholic theologian might present the commitment to a "preferential option for the poor" as a clear sign of the solidarity with the marginalized necessary to form such a situation. A religious commitment to a religion that promotes the search for and acquisition of wisdom on the part of all people would be comprehensively prudent. A religion that blocked such a religious quest would evidently not be prudent.

One example of such a commitment is Gandhi's practice of "satyagraha," clinging to truth or being constant in seeking truth.[13] Gandhi wrote:

> Satyagraha is literally holding on to Truth and it means, therefore, Truth-force. Truth is soul or spirit. It is, therefore, known as soul-force. It excludes the use of violence because man is not capable of knowing the absolute truth, and, therefore, not competent to punish. The word was coined in South Africa to distinguish the non-violent resistance of the Indians of South Africa from the contemporary "passive resistance" of the suffragettes and others. It is not conceived as a weapon of the weak (1964:3).

Gandhi described satyagraha as involving renunciation, hard work, suffering and perhaps death in the service of seeking the truth. Satyagraha is a nonviolent practice wherein "nobody can lose his bearings for long. Directly he takes to the wrong path he stumbles and is thus redirected to the right path" (39).

But the truth Gandhi sought was not the intellectual truths that were a possession of the few disembodied minds. Rather, he sought a practical truth that was shared among all embodied people, a practical truthfulness wherein the voice of the other was heard and the oppression of the other ended. Gandhi suggests a notion of religious practice that requires a radical remapping of the terrain of religious truth—and hence of religious epistemology.

Indeed, for a fully prudent person to make a religious commitment might well require that person to have the goal of remapping the terrain of religious epistemology. In advocating such remapping of academic epistemology, Lorraine Code (1991) noted that epistemically underprivileged people are simply excluded from, erased from, the debates about knowledge and belief. Epistemologists presume that "everyone" has access to information and can develop knowledge. This presumption is, of course, simply false. Code discusses the difficulties women on welfare have in simply acquiring information. She notes how the difficulties they experience are irrelevant to the theories of academic epistemology—and therein lies the problem. The academic map which situates epistemology far from any practical political and social issues is itself the problem. As Code puts it:

As the map is currently drawn, there is no place for analyses of the availability of knowledge, of knowledge-acquisition processes, or—above all—of the political considerations that are implicated in knowing anything more interesting than the fact that the cup is on the table, now. In the received view, availability is purely a contingent matter, knowledge acquisition is a subject for cognitive psychology, and politics should be expunged from analyses of knowledge per se. Practical possibilities and the experiences that reveal them occupy a no-man's land of the not-properly-epistemological. Their particularity, hence their assumed idiosyncrasy, makes them unsuitable candidates for the smoothed-over, unifying analyses that claim territorial supremacy in mainstream epistemology (266).

Code, like Tracy, claims that knowledge is dependent on, although not determined by, the knower's social location (269). One's social location and the factors that contribute to it "limit the constructive process, but they also give it shape. . . . Ecologically rather than individualistically positioned, human beings are interdependent creatures, 'second persons' who rely on one another as much in knowledge as they do for other means of survival"(269). Unlike some communitarians, Code does not romanticize "face-to-face" communities, but recognizes that institutional structures and relationships are necessary for any community to survive. But like Gandhi's implicit revision of what counts as truth in his quest for recognition of the humanity of the oppressed and the acknowledgment of their humanity, so Code's remapping explicitly recognizes the need to engage in shared practices which empower all to have the epistemic skills to acquire access to the information needed to make wise choices.

A religious tradition that recognized this reliance of each upon all and also had an institutional element that not only promoted the extension of the discourse community beyond the epistemically privileged, but also sought to transform the relationships in the community so that all voices could be heard in the communal search for wise religious commitments, would have a claim to being a tradition to which a truly prudent person could subscribe. And such a religion would not have to be standardless; neither Gandhi practically nor Code philosophically are radical relativists. Rather, such a religion would have to involve an institutional and communal commitment both to empower people to speak and to seek a context in which to hear every voice raised. But key is the commitment to, the valorization of the desire for, the formation of the unlimited discourse situation, a situation in which embodied people could speak with each other like Montaigne with his interlocutors, rather than one in which academic minds debate the purely theoretical issues that have little to do with the practical problems that embodied and located people face.

Sharon Welch (1985) has diagnosed the problem as the search for the security seemingly provided by universal and absolute truths, rather than the search for making local and practical truthfulness actual. She writes:

> I have repeatedly found distortions in attempts to produce a universally valid political or theoretical analysis. This leads me to question the principles of political and theoretical analysis, especially the definition of truth. Is a program for political action against patriarchy true if it can be employed by women in any culture, of any race? Are our visions of human community true if they represent the fulfillment of what is essential about all human beings?
>
> I think that the answer to both these questions is no. The ideal of universal or absolute truth is correlated with oppression. I find an openness to many different understandings of truth in the women's movement and in some segments of the peace movement. In sisterhood there is freedom from a self-securing that requires absolutizing one's perspective. In the Christian tradition, however, I find a pathological obsession with security, an obsession that impels the denial of difference (thus concern with heresy and essences), an obsession that leads to a blinding Christian triumphalism, an obsession that receives symbolic expression in the concept of the sovereignty of God (72).

What Welch implicitly calls for is a decentering of the academic practice of religious epistemology, an abandoning of a search for intellectual security (which can never provide practical security), and a turning to openness to differences. This decentering is correlated with a practical epistemology, a seeking of prudent commitments whose wisdom is tempered in the fire of an unlimited discourse community, rather than a quest for absolute truths whose warrant is established among disembodied minds.

Were a theologian's church unwilling or unable to "remap religious epistemology" or to abandon "a blinding Christian triumphalism" presumably that church would be denying the possibility of warranting the wisdom of religious commitment within the space its community and institution constructs. An authentic search for wisdom requires a liberating *praxis* which recognizes how much we rely on each other not only for survival but also for aid and succor in the pursuit of wisdom. To stifle the search or to ignore our fellow-creatures would imply that a fully prudent person could not make such a commitment in that space because such a practice would be in conflict with the practice of seeking wisdom. It would seem obvious that a theologian would properly abandon such practices in tension, as suggested above.

But another path is open. Just as some of the protesters of the Vietnam era sought to reform the practice of patriotism by loving America at its best and refusing to leave it, so the theologian may try to reform ecclesial practice by the unending work of reforming the practices of the church so as to love it at its best and refuse to leave it. That an institution is now defective, that a practice has internal problems, is not *necessarily* a reason to abandon it (although it may be). Insofar as the quest for truth which is not imperialistically universal, but practically local, can be incarnated in a community and an institution, insofar as a reforming or rebelling community can work to undermine institutional oppression, insofar as a tradition can support those who would remap the epistemic situation by bringing all voices to be heard in the ongoing conversation that seeks the life of truthfulness, so might such hope be sufficient to warrant a claim that a prudent religious commitment is possible within such a structure.

Second, the theologian would have to participate in a conversation in which no topics were ruled out of bounds. Obviously, a theologian who could not be prudent$_4$ could not participate in such a discussion, because certain topics could not be discussed without apparently ineradicable role conflict. Those with various prudent$_4$ religious commitments could participate in such a conversation.

For the Catholic theologian a key issue would arise. If institutional authorities made it impossible for theologians to be prudent$_4$, then those authorities are limiting the discourse situations in which theologians can speak as theologians who serve the community and tradition over which the institutional authorities have power. Such authorities would declare that Catholic theologians who differ with them must either withdraw from the ongoing human conversation which is committed to and seeks—even if it cannot realize, fully rational beliefs and prudent commitments, including a commitment to unlimited participation over an unlimited range of topics—or abandon their institutional status as Catholic theologians who serve the tradition for the community. In effect, the authorities would refuse to allow theologians committed to the Catholic tradition to participate in discourse communities that approach *unlimited* discourse situations by *limiting* their ability to speak. This would be an implicit denial of the possibility of a prudent person being committed to Catholicism.

If we seek to have religious commitments that are as prudent as they can be, denying this possibility cannot be appropriate. A religious commitment which precluded participation in a practice that seeks to develop a conversation that is open to all voices could not be made by prudent persons if their religious tradition rules itself or its participants out of the search to understand whether, and which, religious commitments could be prudent or if that tradition excluded voices or erased faces from the conversation. Commitment to a religious tradition could be truly wise only if the tradition, the institution that carries it and the community that practices it empower its participants to attempt to understand whether, and which, religious commitments can be wise.

That a religion did not do so at present might not be reason to abandon it or even a prohibition to take it up. But the mode of relationship to the institution might be rather agonistic and the appropriate social location might have to be that of the rebel. In the Catholic tradition, Friedrich von Hügel might be one model to emulate. He frequently attended Mass, splashed holy water on his head, and sought to keep alive the hope for intellectual and institutional reform within the Church of his time.

The upshot of our analysis is that we cannot give an answer to the question of whether a prudent *person* can be a Catholic theologian. All we can do is explore the very complex territory. But in so doing, we have displayed, for one tradition at a crucial point, the shape of prudential argument and the problems with prudential judgment. At this point, the practical philosopher of religion must stop. Other examples could be adduced, but the issues are clear and the main point should be obvious: to understand the wisdom of religious commitment requires involving oneself in the practices that generate the complex virtue of *phronesis*, practices which I have tried to display here (compare Zagzebski 1993:215–17).

CONCLUSION

This chapter has laid out a different approach to philosophy of religion. The central question is not the abstract one of the rationality of religious belief, but the concrete one of how a practically wise religious person in a specific social location can go about discerning a way to make a religious commitment. Its argument is now concluded: the way to resolve the problem of "religious belief" is not to engage in the disembodied academic practice of seeking universal or unshakable foundations or demonstrating that theistic beliefs are rational, but to engage in the embodied and *necessarily shared* practice of seeking to make and to live out the wisest religious commitments one can. To do so most fully requires a commitment to seek as wise a commitment as one can and to recognize it as well as one can—and that involves a liberating *praxis* which empowers each and all, so far as their social locations and individual abilities allow them, to seek wisdom together. And if some would say that this approach is not philosophy, I would say: what is philosophy at root but the love of wisdom, itself a complex set of practices? And what is the philosophy of religion at root but the desire for wisdom about those interlinked patterns of human relationships that we call religion?

It seems to this philosopher of religion that there are many prudent commitments which religious people can make. We live in different social locations and have different duties to each other, different heritages, and different problems. Our wise commitments and practices will be different. Our paths will properly be different. We may even disagree on whether prudent people can be Catholic theologians. Practically, what else could one expect?

Of course, all too obviously, some paths are or should be closed. Religious commitments that are irrational are unwise. Commitments to traditions that valorize disembodied beliefs and arguments, or commitments that are blind to the embodied multiplicity of people and their perspectives, are unwise. Commitments to practices incarnated in communities and institutions that are irremediably oppressive, triumphalistic, or absolutistic are unwise. Commitments to practices that fail to incorporate working for renewal of traditions, practices, and institutions are unwise. Alas, many religious commitments are apparently unwise as they are taken up in institutions and communities dedicated both to silencing the voices of those who don't fit comfortably in its citadels and cathedrals and to ignoring degrading concommitants, disconfirming evidence, and painful conflicts. But perhaps not all are.

In one sense the book ends here: it is the reader's task to challenge the practice outlined here if it is wrong, to fix it if and where it goes wrong, and, insofar as it is right, to put the plan into practice, to see how the insights developed in one practical investigation can be put into practice in another. The reader must enter into the dialogue.

But in other senses, the book should go on. I am aware of how much is left unsaid, how many discussions have been given short shrift, how many points call for further development. No philosopher of religion, "academic" or "practical," ever has the time or energy to say all he or she could want to say to persuade the reader of his or her view and the wisdom of his or her practice. Our sketches always remain incomplete. The book can't go on in that sense. But the book should also show some practical conclusions its author has reached by trying to put into practice what is described herein. Its epilogue does that.

NOTES TO CHAPTER 5

1. It can also, and more properly, be seen the other way around: Commitment to and participation in the practices of a theistic religion can properly generate theistic belief. But Plantinga's point here, I take it, is not as much the generation of the belief as the warrant for it as a rational belief.

2. Given the distinctions between religious (not epistemological) externalism and internalism made in chapter 1, we can generally take Alston, Plantinga, Malcolm, Phillips and other philosophers of religion to be arguing that religious belief (and, by implication, religious commitment) is warranted for a person. They differ not in finding religious belief finally warrantless, but in whether its warrants are external or internal to religious commitment, religious systems, or religious practices, and on the extent to which a person's practices can be incompatible.

3. Can one make a commitment based on another's experience? Presumably one might sometimes make a commitment based on another's testimony. James suggests that, although one's religious experience may properly warrant one's own beliefs, another's experience and claims provide no warrant for those who do not share the experience: "Those of us who are not personally favored with such specific revelations must stand outside of them altogether and, for the present at least, decide that, since they corroborate incompatible theological doctrines they neutralize one another and leave no fixed results" (1902:399–400). Although Alston has argued for the legitimacy, in general, of a "hearsay" warrant (partly in opposition to James), I find he has not made his case (see Tilley 1992); there is too much contradictory testimony to be heard from religious voices—unless one silences those voices, a practice which, I will argue, is unwise.

4. Katz (1978) hints at this; see also Proudfoot (1985).

5. For example, should a Catholic missionary who belongs to a tradition in which receiving Holy Communion is eating the body of Christ "weaken" the doctrine of transubstantiation into something more symbolic when preaching to a tribe that has a tradition of cannibalism?

6. This example also makes clear that an overriding rule is problematical because the question is what constitutes authentic practice within the tradition.

7. The witness to commitment is not the only duty of theologians, or even their duty in all circumstances; and it is certainly not the duty of theologians only (as opposed to other participants). Still less does it imply that they must show that participation in other religions is unwise—indeed such an attempt would itself be unwise. Yet this overarching duty is at least analogous to David Tracy's claim, "The characteristic which distinguishes theology as a discipline from religious studies, moreover, is the fact that scholars in religious studies may legitimately confine their interests to 'meaning' while theologians must by the intrinsic demands of their discipline face the questions of both meaning and truth" (1981:20). If Tracy is correct, then the overall practical issue for theologians is the wisdom of religious commitment.

8. Some would argue that engagement in these disciplines requires no commitment to a religious tradition. I agree, assuming that such a "theologian" would only be working in the academy and contributing to the church only as an "outsider."

9. I appreciate discussions with Dermot Lane which helped me to see the relevance of this point.

10. As it is not clear how, or if, Malcolm distinguishes the process, disposition, or act of believing from the content of religious belief, it is not clear that the examples are true parallels, for one can distinguish the propositional content, "My name is N. N." from what I do in believing my name to be N. N. I have tried to interpret Malcolm's work in a manner appropriate for the present investigation. For an evaluation of his approach, see Penelhum 1986:227–237.

11. I have unabashedly assimilated the work of religiously committed philosophers of religion to the work of theologians in this section. In the context of defending the reasonableness of religious belief or commitment, the philosopher of religion is functioning at least as a quasi-theologian or a rational theologian.

12. It is a commonplace among Roman Catholic scholars that numerous theologians take positions on controversial issues that are as daringly "unorthodox" as those of the theologians cited. Why does the CDF not investigate the others? The most plausible answer is that the CDF attends to theologians who have an influential position in the academy and who can thus influence others. But these theologians have such influence, at least in part, because they are recognized for their excellence as scholars and teachers.

13. These paragraphs extend an earlier argument I made for "satyagraha" as embodying a standard of truth for calling a story true in the context of judging religious narratives (see Tilley 1985:208–210).

Epilogue

A Practical Conclusion

At the end of chapter 3, I claimed that we must solve the problem of many practices if we are to solve the real problem of the rationality of religious belief. Since then we have been engaging in the practical philosophy of religion as I promised in chapter 1. But it seems that all we have found along the way is more problems.

I claimed in chapter 1 that the burning religious question is a practical one. Now, at the end, I can't give you the final answer because the answer is also a practical one. One displays the wisdom of religious commitment in living it. You have given your answer. You are walking your path. Your wager has been made. Is it a wise one? In the view propounded here, if we have entered into the shared philosophical practice of seeking the wisdom of religious commitment and if we enter into the shared religious practices of committed seeking Wisdom in the tradition of Pascal and Montaigne, it is. And yet our paths may be irreducibly different.

Perhaps all the religions and the practices they carry fall short in actuality. Perhaps many offer only hope for a prudent religious practice. None can finally or infallibly form a person not only with a taste for the ultimate as that tradition defines it but also with a taste for a divine Wisdom. Perhaps each tradition has substantial deformations, especially by the social evils of racism, sexism, and patriarchal forms of hierarchicalism. Because this is so, there is surely substantial room for the practical agnostics who walk away from all these traditions and seek to find their own path apart from these institutionally carried traditions. Their positive commitments, their seeking after what is true, good, and beautiful, may often display a taste for divine wisdom more fully than the search that religious practitioners pursue. But these paths are not above the battle (as Flew seems to think); rather, they are part of the agonistic conversation about the wisdom of religious commitment.

Moreover, the commitment must be a practical one, not merely a theoretical one. Sharon Welch following Anthony Giddens (whom she also quotes) points out that what makes the conversation possible is not the search for consensus, but the commitment to solidarity. People can be in solidarity despite a lack of consensus. She puts it this way:

> Giddens poses a thought-provoking alternative to Habermas: " 'Our first sentence,' you once wrote, 'expresses unequivocally the intention of universal and unconstrained consensus.' Why not say that our first gesture of recognition of another person promises a universal solidarity of human beings?"
> The intention of universal solidarity is potentially more inclusive and more transformative than is the goal of consensus. Many liberation ethicists argue that the search for consensus is a continuation of the dream of domination (Welch 1990:132–33).

The community must not only give lip service to "consensus." That practice can too easily and surreptitiously continue the dream of domination by seeking consensus "on our terms." Rather, in all our conversations we must recognize the "otherness" of each other and must hear their voices even if consensus is not reached.

I have argued that we can see better and worse practices, carried in better and worse traditions, guided by better and worse institutions, and incarnated in better and worse communities. We can see the complexity of the virtue of *phronesis* both in "morality" and "religion." The better religions promote and the worse ones obstruct those who dwell within them from acquiring that taste for Wisdom. The better religions allow the others to be different and to question those who dwell within them; the worse ones remake the image of the other to fit "our" views and never allow "them" to question "our" terms. The better ones find room for difference even in the face of institutional authority, while the worse ones require everyone to walk lockstep or leave the tradition.

We can harvest finally some of the insights of Montaigne with which we began. If our wager is wise, we can participate with joy and fervor in the practice of agonistic conversation. Those who claim that God is on their side or that they are on God's side because God intervenes in the war they carry on to destroy the individual bodies and the body of tradition their opponents carry cannot be comprehensively wise (see Scarry 1985). They constrict and destroy the discourse community and the traditions that can be brought into conversation. In effect, they refuse to wager on Wisdom. They refuse to allow Wisdom to emerge in the conversation of many different voices. Their bets are on power, that might is right for them no matter what it does to others. Their ideology can be unmasked, if not overthrown (see Tilley 1995, part 3).

Of course, it is unwise to live in some communities, to be subject to some institutions, and to engage in some practices. Communities and institutions that stifle wise practices or that carry a tradition supporting unwise practices should be fled. If one can leave them, one should. If one can't or won't, the wise commitment becomes a practice of working to reform, overthrow, or undermine them. The fact that almost no contemporary Catholic theologians have been excommunicated (even though some have been disciplined) leaves the Catholic room for hope that a religious commitment in the Roman Catholic context may well be made by a prudent person; indeed, such hope is true for many, but not all, religious traditions. Yet there is room for disagreement here and for continuing the conversation to try to discover together where wisdom lies.

Our situation is somewhat different from Pascal's. Our options are not for true heathenism and true religion. The argument here shows that there are many paths which can realize a commitment to that than which a greater cannot be conceived. We have the problem of many practices. But it is not fully intact. Proper beliefs arise from, and are generated by, the practices that constitute the love of that than which a greater cannot be conceived. If this analysis is correct, then the problems for religious epistemology generated by religious diversity cannot be theoretically resolved, but must be practically dissolved by participation in a Montaignian conversation. A commitment to the practice of unlimited truthfulness and peaceableness that includes all who would become aware of their own wagers is a practical constituent of the religious commitment to that than which a greater cannot be conceived. It is unwise to be committed to institutions or communities that fail to have such a commitment as a constituent of their religious tradition.

What is a situated person to do? Exactly as we have been doing: learning how to become wise about religious commitment. The practice of seeking a wise religious commitment begins with unconstrained conversation. To use McClendon's definition of a practice, the end of this practice is religious wisdom. Its practitioners begin wherever they are. We differ from the points at which we start and the paths we walk. Other people will begin in other places. Within the practice, different people may find widely different paths to be live options. Perhaps some will find themselves with more than two live options. But why expect otherwise? The real world is messy. What practitioners have in common is that we enter the conversation not as disinterested academics, but as engaged believers, perhaps even engaged nihilist, atheist, agnostic, or "heathen" believers; we enter into it with the desire to find that which is true, good, beautiful and wise and to enable all to seek fulfillment of the same desire in their different ways. Those who do not seek wisdom need not join the conversation. But who are they? Those who refuse to think about their lives and commitments, who prefer the unexamined life or who prefer power to Wisdom. Those who refuse to recognize the shape of the wager or who choose to continue to be committed to a finite good.

Once we recognize that we do wager, then our work uses various means governed by practical rules to narrow our choices to the most plausible ones. But the plausibility we seek is not only a noetic matter, but also a contextual one of taste, attraction and affect, a matter for shared exploration. As Jaggar (1989) wrote, "Emotions prompt us to act appropriately, to approach some people and situations and to avoid others, to caress or cuddle, fight or flee. Without emotion, human life would be unthinkable" (154). The end is to enable all to embody the best available practices in our lives, practices affectively attractive and intellectually satisfying. Any tradition that fails to empower and to draw in those who are not (yet) in position to participate in the practice of seeking what is true, creating what is beautiful, and doing what is good should be avoided. The traditions that empower people to do and to seek truth, beauty, and goodness are constituted, in part, by an authentic "peaceableness." As Code finds academic epistemology inadequate because of its failure to include social and political aspects, so I would claim that a religious tradition that did not include practices designed to overcome the marginalization and dislocation of those without privilege or position cannot be authentically "peaceable" and thus a candidate for that best practice.

If the authorities in a tradition show that commitment in that tradition cannot be comprehensively wise, then anybody who seeks to be prudent cannot make a commitment to and in that tradition unless it is to reform or rebel. Prudent commitment is impossible in embodied traditions that oppose the search for wisdom, fail to empower people, or limit the voices to be heard. The institutional authorities in the Roman Catholic Church all too often abuse their authority and seem willing to join the fideists. If they attack the institutional roles of "errant" theologians rather than engaging in Montaignian discourse with them, they undercut the possibility of finding commitment to Catholic Christianity prudent. For some, their acts show the wisdom of abandoning the Church. The institutional authorities often do not live by an authentic peaceableness; instead, they choose to use power to settle disputes about the tradition.

However, the corruptions of institutional power do not necessarily infect the local communities that communicate the tradition. Even if the institutional authorities abuse their power, the parishes, base communities, religious orders, guilds and other associations that are Catholics' practical religious homes can be communities of solidarity and resistance, of joy and celebration. While I recognize that others properly make other prudential judgments, mine has been, and remains, to live with the tensions.

But I am constantly challenged by the commitments of those who leave the institution and community to seek wisdom in other places. All too often, they have had their faith beat out of them. If the argument made here is correct, to remain in Catholicism requires that I take a stance that seeks to reform abuses of power or at least to reveal their ideological bases. I can seek to mitigate its effects in the locations in which I live and work, sustained by the hope of preserving and extending the valued practices carried in the tradition. Like Moshe's friend in chapter 2, I may not be much of a slave-rescuing type, but not everyone has to walk the same path, only head in a wise direction. Others will have to consider the wisdom of commitment to Tibetan Buddhism, Shi'ite Islam, Methodist Christianity, or secular humanism. And because each starts in different place, we may well come to different choices. Nevertheless, the practices we properly undertake in varied religious traditions may be analogous so that we may come in different ways to different forms of endless happiness and joy, if not to the same belief.

The development of a practical philosophy of religion is an analogue of the wager argument. The wise person will choose to be part of a tradition that has antecedent appeal to one, as well as the central and distinctive practice of love or devotion to that than which a greater cannot be conceived. Such devotion will be tradition-specific and particular, but it will also have a universalizing goal and intent, not of oppression, but of solidarity, especially solidarity in conversation. And by engaging in practical conversation, members of such traditions can come to practical agreement without having to silence the voices of the other by claiming to have formulated universal truths. We can come to mutual enlightenment.

I note with joy the very happy chance that "Buddha is a Catholic saint." He is inscribed in the Roman martyrology. He was canonized as St. Josaphat whose life story manifested the asceticism and devotion of an Enlightened one, a boddhisattva, a Buddha in practice. The influence of that story on Tolstoy (Almond 1987), the well-known influences of Tolstoy on Gandhi, and of Gandhi on M. L. King, Jr., witnesses to the fact that even if we cannot agree in theory, we can share common practices and recognize the beauty, wisdom, and goodness that others generate. Perhaps, in the messy world of particular commitments, more cannot be sought, certainly not in theory.

Works Cited

I have generally cited works to their author (not their translator) and to the first available publication in English. If the edition actually cited is not the first publication, the date of the edition cited is found at the end of the entry.

Adams, Robert M.
1987 *The Virtue of Faith and Other Essays in Philosophical Theology*. New York: Oxford University Press.

Almond, Philip C.
1987. "The Buddha of Christendom: A Review of the Legend of Barlaam and Josaphat." *Religious Studies* 23:391–406.

Alston, William P.
1982. "Religious Experience and Religious Belief." *Nous* 16:3–12
1991. *Perceiving God: The Epistemology of Religious Experience*. Ithaca: Cornell University Press.
1994. "Response to My Critics." *Religious Studies* 30(2):171–80.

Berger, Peter
1967. *The Sacred Canopy: Elements of a Sociological Theory of Religion*. Garden City, NY: Doubleday Anchor Books, 1967.

Boone, Kathleen C.
1989. *The Bible Tells Them So: The Discourse of Protestant Fundamentalism*. Albany: SUNY Press.

Bowker, John
1970. *Problems of Suffering in Religions of the World*. Cambridge: Cambridge University Press.

Brown, Stuart C., ed.
1977. *Reason and Religion*. Ithaca: Cornell University Press.

Clebsch, William A.
1979. *Christianity in European History*. New York: Oxford University Press.

Clifford, William K.
1877. "The Ethics of Belief." In *The Ethics of Belief Debate*, ed. Gerald McCarthy, 19–36. AAR Studies in Religion 41. Atlanta: Scholars Press, 1986.

Code, Lorraine
1991. *What Can She Know? Feminist Theory and the Construction of Knowledge*. Ithaca: Cornell University Press.
1994. "Responsibility and Rhetoric." *Hypatia* 9(1):1–20.

D'Arcy, Eric
1991. "The Universal Catechism and Anglo-American Philosophy." *Living Light* 27(2):140–50.
Dawkins, Richard
1986. *The Blind Watchmaker*. New York: W. W. Norton and Co.
Denzinger, H., and A. Schonmetzer
DS *Enchiridion Symbolorum, definitionum et declarationum de rebus fide et morum*. 35th ed. New York: Kenedy.
Farley, Edward
1990. *Good and Evil: Interpreting a Human Condition*. Minneapolis: Fortress Press.
Flew, Antony G. N.
1955. "Theology and Falsification." In *New Essays in Philosophical Theology*, ed. Antony Flew and Alasdair MacIntyre, 96–99, 105–8. New York: Macmillan, 1970.
1966. *God and Philosophy*. New York: Harcourt, Brace and World.
1976. *The Presumption of Atheism*. New York: Harper and Row.
1985. "The Burden of Proof." In *Knowing Religiously*, ed. Leroy Rouner, 103–15. Notre Dame: University of Notre Dame Press.
Gallagher, Eugene V.
1993. "Conversion and Community in Late Antiquity." *Journal of Religion* 73(1):1–15.
Gandhi, Mohandas K.
1964. *Gandhi on Non-Violence*, ed. Thomas Merton. New York: New Directions.
Geertz, Clifford
1973. *The Interpretation of Cultures*. New York: Basic Books.
Geivett, R. Douglas and Brendan Sweetman, eds.
1992. *Contemporary Perspectives on Religious Epistemology*. New York: Oxford University Press.
Goldman, Alvin I.
1986. *Epistemology and Cognition*. Cambridge, MA: Harvard University Press.
Greco, John
1993. "Is Natural Theology Necessary for Theistic Knowledge?" In *Rational Faith: Catholic Responses to Reformed Epistemology*, ed. Linda Zagzebski, 168–98. Notre Dame: University of Notre Dame Press.
Habermas, Jürgen
1983. "Modernity—An Incomplete Project." In *The Anti-Aesthetic: Essays in Post-Modern Culture*, ed. Hal Foster, 3–15. Port Townsend, WA: Washington Bay Press.
1987. *The Theory of Commnicative Action*, trans. Thomas McCarthy. Vol. 2, *Lifeworld and System*. Boston: Beacon.
Hammarskjöld, Dag
1964. *Markings*, trans. Leif Sjoberg and W. H. Auden. London: Faber and Faber.

Harvey, Van A.
  1966. *The Historian and the Believer*. New York: Macmillan.
  1979. "The Ethics of Belief Reconsidered." In *The Ethics of Belief Debate*, ed. Gerald McCarthy, 189–203. AAR Studies in Religion 41. Atlanta: Scholars Press, 1986.
Hick, John
  1964. *The Existence of God*. New York: Macmillan.
  1989. *An Interpretation of Religion: Human Responses to the Transcendent*. New Haven: Yale University Press.
Hügel, Friedrich von
  1904. "Official Authority and Living Religion." In *Essays and Addresses on the Philosophy of Religion*. Second Series, 3–23. London: J. M. Dent, 1926.
Hume, David
  1777. *An Inquiry Concerning Human Understanding*, ed. Charles W. Hendel. Indianapolis: Bobbs Merrill, 1976.
  1779. *Dialogues Concerning Natural Religion*, ed. Norman Kemp Smith. New York: Macmillan, 1989.
Jaggar, Alison M.
  1989. "Love and Knowledge: Emotion in Feminist Epistemology." In *Gender/Body/Knowledge: Feminist Reconstructions of Being and Knowing*, ed. Alison M. Jaggar and Susan R. Bordo. New Brunswick, NJ: Rutgers University Press.
James, William
  1896. "The Will to Believe." In *The Ethics of Belief Debate*, ed. Gerald McCarthy, 55–72. AAR Studies in Religion 41. Atlanta: Scholars Press, 1986.
  1902. *The Varieties of Religious Experience*. New York: Macmillan, 1961.
Katz, Steven T.
  1978. "Language, Epistemology and Mysticism." In *Mysticism and Philosophical Analysis*, ed. Steven T. Katz, 22–74. New York: Oxford University Press.
Knitter, Paul
  1985. *No Other Name: A Critical Survey of Christian Attitudes Toward the World Religions*. Maryknoll, NY: Orbis Books.
Kornblith, Hilary
  1985. "Introduction: What is Naturalistic Epistemology?" In *Naturalizing Epistemology*, ed. Hilary Kornblith, 1–13. Cambridge: MIT Press.
Lash, Nicholas
  1988. *Easter in Ordinary: Reflections on the Human Experience and the Knowledge of God*. Charlottesville: University of Virginia Press.
Lindbeck, George
  1984. *The Nature of Doctrine*. Philadelphia: Westminster Press.
Lycan, William G. and George N. Schlesinger
  1989. "You Bet Your Life: Pascal's Wager Defended." In *Contemporary Perspectives on Religious Epistemology*, ed. R. Douglas Geivett and Brendan Sweetman, 270–82. New York: Oxford University Press, 1992.
MacIntyre, Alasdair
  1984. *After Virtue*. 2d. ed. Notre Dame: University of Notre Dame Press.

Mackie, John L.

1982. *The Miracle of Theism: Arguments for and against the Existence of God.* Oxford: Clarendon Press.

Malcolm, Norman

1977. "The Groundlessness of Belief." In *Reason and Religion*, ed. Stuart C. Brown, 143–57. Ithaca: Cornell University Press.

Mavrodes, George

1982. "Belief, Porportionality and Probability." In *Reason and Decision: Studies in Applied Philosophy*, ed. Michael Bradie and Kenneth Sayre, 58–68. Bowling Green: Applied Philosophy Program.

1986. "Intellectual Morality in Clifford and James." In *The Ethics of Belief Debate*, ed. Gerald McCarthy, 205–19. AAR Studies in Religion 41. Atlanta: Scholars Press.

McClendon, James Wm., Jr.

1986. *Ethics: Systematic Theology, Volume I.* Nashville: Abingdon.

1994. *Doctrines: Systematic Theology, Volume II.* Nashville: Abingdon.

McCarthy, Gerald D.

1982. "Meaning, Morals, and the Existence of God." *Horizons* 9:288–301.

Metz, Johann Baptist

1981. *The Emergent Church: The Future of Christianity in a Postbourgeois World*, trans. Peter Mann. New York: Crossroad.

Morris, Thomas V.

1986a. *The Logic of God Incarnate.* Ithaca: Cornell University Press.

1986b. "Pascalian Wagering." In *Contemporary Perspectives on Religious Epistemology*, ed. R. Douglas Geivett and Brendan Sweetman, 257–269. New York: Oxford University Press, 1992.

1992. *Making Sense of it All: Pascal and the Meaning of Life.* Grand Rapids: Eerdmanns.

Montaigne, Michel de

1958. *The Complete Essays of Montaigne*, trans. Donald M. Frame. Stanford: Stanford University Press.

Murdoch, Iris

1970. *The Sovereignty of Good.* London: Routledge.

Nagel, Thomas

1993. "The Mind Wins." *New York Review of Books.* March 4.

Newman, John Henry

1870. *The Grammar of Assent.* Garden City: Doubleday, 1955.

Niebuhr, H. Richard

1944. *The Meaning of Revelation.* New York: Macmillan.

Nielsen, Kai

1971. *Contemporary Critiques of Religion.* New York: Herder.

1973. *Ethics Without God.* London: Pemberton.

1985. "God and Coherence: On the Epistemological Foundations of Religious Belief." In *Knowing Religiously*, ed. Leroy Rouner, 89–102. Notre Dame: University of Notre Dame Press.

Nock, Arthur Darby
1933. *Conversion: The Old and the New in Religion from Alexander the Great to Augustine of Hippo*. Oxford: Oxford University Press.
Pascal, Blaise
1958. *Pascal's Pensees*, trans. G. F. Trotter. Introduction by T. S. Eliot. New York: E. P. Dutton.
Penelhum, Terence
1983. *God and Skepticism*. Boston: Reidel.
1986. "Do Religious Beliefs need Grounds?" *Nederlands Theologisch Tijdschrift* (July) 227–37.
Phillips, Dewi Zephaniah
1988. *Faith after Foundationalism*. London: Routledge.
Plantinga, Alvin
1974. *God, Freedom and Evil*. New York: Harper and Row.
1981. "Is Belief in God Properly Basic?" *Nous* 15(1):41–52.
1983. "Reason and Belief in God." In *Faith and Rationality*, ed. Alvin Plantinga and Nicholas Wolterstorff, 16–93. Notre Dame: University of Notre Dame Press.
1993a. *Warrant: The Current Debate*. New York: Oxford University Press.
1993b. *Warrant and Proper Function*. New York: Oxford University Press.
Proudfoot, Wayne
1985. *Religious Experience*. Berkeley: University of California.
Quine, W. V. O., and J. S. Ullian
1978. *The Web of Belief*. 2d Ed. New York: Random House.
Ramsey, Ian T.
1957. *Religious Language: An Empirical Placing of Theological Phrases*. London: SCM Press.
Ratté, John
1968. *Three Modernists: Alfred Loisy, George Tyrrell, William L. Sullivan*. London: Sheed and Ward.
Rocca, Gregory P.
1986. "The Existence of God in Hans Küng's *Does God Exist?*" *Faith and Philosophy* 3:177–191.
Rorty, Richard
1989. *Contingency, Irony and Solidarity*. Cambridge: Cambridge University Press.
Russell, Bertrand
1903. "The Free Man's Worship." In *Why I Am Not a Christian*, 104–16. London: Allen and Unwin, 1957.
Scarry, Elaine
1985. *The Body in Pain: The Making and Unmaking of the World*. New York: Oxford University Press.
Schreiter, Robert S.
1985. *Constructing Local Theologies*. Maryknoll: Orbis Books.
Searle, John
1992. *The Rediscovery of the Mind*. Cambridge: MIT Press.

Short, Larry Ray

1992. "In a Poetic Fashion." Ph.D. dissertation, Tallahassee: Florida State University.

Stark, Rodney, and William Sims Bainbridge

1985. *The Future of Religion: Secularization, Revival and Cult Formation*. Berkeley: University of California Press.

Stich, Stephen

1990. *The Fragmentation of Reason*. Cambridge: MIT Press.

Swinburne, Richard

1977. *The Coherence of Theism*. Oxford: Clarendon Press.

1979. *The Existence of God*. Oxford: Clarendon Press

1981. *Faith and Reason*. Oxford: Clarendon Press.

Thiel, John

1991. *Imagination and Authority: Theological Authorship in the Modern Tradition*. Minneapolis: Augsburg/Fortress Press.

Tilley, Terrence W.

1978. *Talking of God: An Introduction to Philosophical Analysis of Religious Language*. New York: Paulist Press.

1985. *Story Theology*. Wilmington, Del: Michael Glazier.

1989. "The Prudence of Religious Commitment." *Horizons* 16(1):45–64.

1990. "Reformed Epistemology and Religious Fundamentalism: How Basic Are Our Basic Beliefs?" *Modern Theology* 6(3):237–57.

1991. *The Evils of Theodicy*. Washington, DC: Georgetown University Press.

1992. "Reformed Epistemology in a Jamesian Perspective." *Horizons* 19(1):84–98.

1994. "The Institutional Element in Religious Experience." *Modern Theology* 10(2):185–212.

1995. *Postmodern Theologies and the Challenge of Religious Diversity*. Maryknoll, NY: Orbis Books.

Toulmin, Stephen

1992. *Cosmopolis: The Hidden Agenda of Modernity*. New York: Free Press.

Tracy, David

1981. *The Analogical Imagination*. New York: Crossroad.

Weber, Max

1947. *The Theory of Social and Economic Organization*, trans. A. M. Henderson and Talcott Parsons. New York: Oxford University Press.

1958. *The Protestant Ethic and the Spirit of Capitalism*, trans. Talcott Parsons. New York: Charles Scribner's Sons.

Welch, Sharon

1985. *Communities of Solidarity and Resistance*. Maryknoll, NY: Orbis Books.

1990. *A Feminist Ethic of Risk*. Philadelphia: Fortress Press.

Wiesel, Elie

1960. *Night*, trans. Stella Rodway. New York: Bantam Books, 1986.

Woodward, Kenneth

1993. "The Rites of Americans." *Newsweek*. November 29:80–82.

Zagzebski, Linda

1993. "Religious Knowledge and the Virtues of the Mind." In *Rational Faith: Catholic Responses to Reformed Epistemology*, ed. Linda Zagzebski, 199–225. Notre Dame: University of Notre Dame Press.

Index